WHAT OT

"The Bible comes alive when we realize that the men and woman mentioned in its pages were flesh and blood just like us. Scared, imperfect, flesh-driven humans, yet deeply loved by our Father. Mike Tison has skillfully, and in an honest down-to-earth fashion, shared how God has always loved and used flawed mankind. Be encouraged as you read *Reluctant Misfits* and come away with a greater confidence in HIM and your story within HIS plan."

– Tom Roy, Founder & President of Unlimited Potential, Inc.

"God has big plans for all of us! For some reason we let sin, fear and doubt stop us from following God's call. In Mike Tison's new book, *Reluctant Misfits*, he provides a first person narrative of some of the greatest heroes found throughout the Bible. While each man wasn't perfect and battled sin, God used them in a historic, powerful way. And he wants to use you too. Mike's new book is a must read! It will have a profound effect on anyone who has a passion to be a warrior for Christ."

– Lane Walker, Award-winning Author & Keynote Speaker

"In *Reluctant Misfits*, readers will find the motivation and encouragement they need to move forward in the purpose God has for their lives. Mike uses a sequence of stories to develop the theme for each chapter. We read about a man who happened to have his story told in Scripture, followed by the author's sharing of his own personal experience, followed by another inspiring faith story. Each of these stories are about flawed men, who God used to bring hope to a lost world. If you are questioning your purpose in life, or are frustrated and disappointed with the seemingly impossible odds against you, read this book. And, if you feel as if life is good and everything is going well for you, then read *Reluctant Misfits* to help you inspire others with these stories that build faith, perseverance, courage and hope.

—Cheryl Bongiorno, Author of *Finding Jesus in Jeremiah*
www.cherylbongiorno.com

RELUCTANT MISFITS

Hope for the Men God Chooses

MIKE TISON

Reluctant Misfits

Cover design by Laura Drew
Interior layout design by Katherine Lloyd, The DESK

ISBN: 978-0-578-14932-5

Library of Congress Control Number: 2015900506

Printed in the United States of America

DEDICATION

This book is dedicated to my five amazing children: Kayla, Zachary, Seth, Micah, and Lydia.

Know that God loves you and that He has a plan for your lives. Always follow Him and commit to Him with passion! Each of you is gifted in special ways. Learn your gifts and use them to help build God's kingdom. Always remember that God uses weak men and women to do great things for Him, so don't strive to be perfect; just be available, obedient, and willing. — Love, Dad.

CONTENTS

INTRODUCTION

A struggle rages deep inside me. It is not a war for my soul, as that victory has already been won. Instead, it is a fight against the darkness that I so easily embrace. There can be only one winner. The darkness that I cling to is filled with sin, doubt, insecurity, and fear. One day, I hope to be free from this bondage, but deep down I realize that it is going to take a lifetime of struggle to overcome this opponent. I spend too much time battling with myself, opening up old feelings of being unqualified, unworthy, and that God could never use a man like me.

> *You will never not be afraid so don't wait for the fear to go away. I think too many men feel faith-walking is a "fear-free" experience. It is not. Dealing with fear while walking in faith is the norm and there is something comforting about that — Sr. Pastor Paul Bauman, Trinity Church, Holdrege, NE.*

Buried in me is a real understanding of the promises of God. I've seen firsthand how God has moved in my life in ways that cannot be explained, yet I retreat when I should be moving forward. I know that my Creator has the power to do great things through me if I could only commit myself to Him with unwavering faith. Yet, I sit when an adventure awaits.

> *Go for it. Make some mistakes, but keep trying new things, as long as it fits into the things God has called us to do — Sr. Pastor Doug Schmidt, Woodside Bible Church, Troy, MI.*

This battle never seems to end. I sin when I should conquer; I boast when I should be humble. I'm a weak man. I should be stronger. I'm fortunate that God never gets tired of dragging me out of the morasses of life. I'm aware of the power of the Holy Spirit to be able to take on the world, yet fear inside causes me to cower like a beaten man.

I know I am not alone. The Bible is filled with stories of men who have felt this way. Is it enough to know that He loves me? Is it enough to know He still chooses me even after I come to the realization of who I really am?

I know God loves me and has a unique plan for my life, but I feel compelled to compare my adventure to others. I continually set aside God's grace to devour a life of man-made expectations. Those shiny idols draw my attention away from the loving Savior. As I fall short, I'm left with nothing but the thought that I'm just a weak man, a reluctant misfit. Why would God use a misfit like me?

Men like me, who come from ordinary circumstances, who don't feel qualified to do the things God asks, are reluctant misfits who are standing in the way of God's plans; but in the end we are willing, available, and obedient.

> *All God's giants have been weak men who did great things for God because they reckoned on His being with them — James Hudson Taylor.*

God's ways are higher than my ways. He has reasons for what He chooses. It may not make sense to me, or to others, but God knows, and that should be good enough for me.

With the following stories, take time to reflect on the type of man you are. Where have you come from? Where do you want to go? Who do you want to become and how do you relate to the characters?

It is my hope that you will be strengthened in your faith and you will realize that you don't have to be perfect to be used by God. Be encouraged. Desire Him first and foremost and be willing, available, and obedient.

> *Start serving Christ wholeheartedly where you are right now — Major League Baseball chaplain.*

Chapter One

MANSLAUGHTER

The body wasn't easy to drag. While his muscular frame had barely any body fat, he was heavier than he looked, and to make matters worse, there was hardly enough sand to bury his long form. Under the circumstances it would have to do; besides, this man didn't deserve a proper burial, not after what he did to those slaves.

Sleeping last night was difficult, but the consolation of exacting my own justice on this brutal taskmaster assuaged any guilt creeping into my soul. He got what was coming to him; for that reason I'd be able to easily put the murder behind me, or so I thought. Tending to my royal duties the following day, I encountered a slave beating another slave. Confronting the assailant, I scolded him. "Why do you strike your companion?" His response surprised me, "Who made you a prince and a judge over us? Do you mean to kill me as you killed the taskmaster?" His statement pierced my soul. I was a killer and a hypocrite.

What have I done? If these slaves know what happened then it is only a matter of time before word spreads to Pharaoh and then my death at the hands of the Egyptians. Panic set in and fear prodded me to flee.

There was no plan of escape as I fled from Egypt to the east and into the desert wilderness. Could I escape the guilt of my sin? Would I be able to start afresh or will my past continue to haunt me? Little did I know that God was already beginning to use my past to shape my future.

Exhausted and tired from travelling, I pressed on. God's provision was perfect as I stumbled across a well at just the right time and drank the fresh water. For the first time in quite a while I was able to rest, but the peace I found there wouldn't last for long.

As I was reclining against the well, silence gave way to a thunderous rumble of two approaching herds. The first flock to arrive was tended by seven young women. The second flock was driven by yelling male shepherds trying to force the women's flock away. The shepherds were intimidating the women, trying to chase them from the well.

I'm not sure why, but I stood up. My confrontation with those arrogant sheep-herders didn't go well for them. After safeguarding the rights of these women, I felt I should help them water their flocks. This was not the type of work I was used to doing in Egypt. I could only imagine the looks I'd get from the royal family. But for some strange reason my heart was no longer concerned with my lavish Egyptian lifestyle. A tiny spark ignited inside me and its flames were now licking at the edges of my heart. Burning into my soul was a strong desire to protect and deliver the innocent from oppression. Three words repeatedly rang through my soul: justice, deliverance, and salvation. Where was this coming from?

After the women's animals were watered and cared for, I sent them on their way. As they left, I couldn't stop thinking about one woman who seemed to match my gaze with her own soft but probing stare. The sun had been kind to her tanned complexion and her eyes were a powerful attraction. The way she carried herself made me think that I would like to meet her again.

After all the commotion died down, I reclined again against the well, letting the events of the past few days play out in my thoughts. I wondered if God would ever forgive me or if He would just discard me. At first my mind began to whirl as I tried sorting out the answers to these questions, then, realizing I didn't have any answers, my mind slowed and I drifted off to sleep.

I'm not sure exactly how much time passed before I was awakened by a soft female voice. The woman sheepherder with whom I had been so infatuated was standing over me inviting me to come and visit her father. She said that he wanted to thank me for standing up for his daughters and protecting them. It wasn't necessary, but how could I say no to her? She was beautiful, and who wouldn't want a chance to spend more time getting to know this woman who was beginning to steal my heart? Most likely there would be a reception with food. After being alone in the wilderness for so long, I could use the company and some sustenance.

One of the seven daughters told me their father was the high priest of Midian. His name was Reuel, but everyone called him Jethro. He was a great host, and later I would learn that he was also a great man. During the reception he thanked me for helping his daughters and made me a proposal. He appreciated my sense of duty and protection, so he offered me a position to help with his flocks and to be a part of their family for as long as I liked. It was an offer I easily agreed to. After all, there were things here to hold my interest and the food was great; most importantly, it just felt as though I could call this place home.

Over time I did a lot to help out Jethro's family and grew attached to his daughter Zipporah. He gave her to me in marriage;

and after we had a son we named him Gershom, which means, "I have been a sojourner in a foreign land." Life was good but it wasn't an easy life, and often I thought about my purpose for existing.

Being a shepherd was rewarding and it was great to be a part of such a supportive and loving family. Although keeping the flock does have its challenges and dangers, I was unprepared for an encounter that was about to change my life.

Jethro's flock was positioned on the western side of the wilderness where I was responsible for shepherding it. I came to a place called Horeb, known as the mountain of God, when all of a sudden something caught my attention: a nearby bush ignited on fire. The flame wasn't normal. It possessed an iridescent quality and was filled with vibrant colors, yet it didn't burn up like a normal bush fire. It wasn't blazing hot, but warm and inviting. It was majestic and all-consuming, but nothing disintegrated. I realized that it was the angel of the Lord calling to me from the flaming bush.

"Moses, Moses!" the flame called out to me. I responded, "Here I am." Then He said, "Do not come near; take your sandals off your feet, for the place on which you stand is holy ground. I am the God of your fathers: the God of Abraham, the God of Isaac, and the God of Jacob." I hid my face. I was afraid. I did not want to look at God.

The Lord told me that He had seen the affliction of His people, my people in Egypt, and had heard their cry because of their treatment by their taskmasters. He told me He knew their suffering and had come to deliver them out of the Egyptians' hands. He went on to describe a land in which He was going to bless them. He explained that it was a good and broad land, a land flowing with milk and honey. Then what He said next surprised me: "And now, behold the cry of the people of Israel has come to me, and I have also seen the oppression with which the Egyptians oppress them.

Come, I will send you to Pharaoh that you may bring my people, the children of Israel, out of Egypt."

I was in shock. The Lord God had just asked me to go to Pharaoh and deliver His people. What? I asked Him, "Who am I that I should go to Pharaoh and bring the children of Israel out of Egypt?"

"Moses," He replied, "I will be with you, and this shall be the sign for you, that I have sent you: when you have brought the people out of Egypt, you shall serve God on this mountain."

My brain was trying to comprehend all that had been said to me. I asked him, "If I come to the people of Israel and say to them, 'The God of your fathers has sent me to you,' and they ask me, 'What is his name?' what shall I say to them?"

I never should have asked that question. His response was loud, sharp, and bold. "I AM WHO I AM." He gave me instructions and told me that He would stretch out His hand and strike Egypt with all kinds of wonders. He assured me that they would let us go.

It was unsettling and may have been too much for me. I thought of every way I could to try and get out of doing it, but God had other plans. When I told him that Pharaoh wouldn't believe me, He told me to throw my staff down on the ground. Instantly it turned into a serpent. I began to run but he stopped me with His commanding voice and told me to pick it up. Immediately it returned to being a wooden staff. He also told me to put my hand inside my cloak. As I slowly pulled it out, I could see skin lesions and sores covering my hand and wrist. My jaw dropped. I slid my hand back in, pulled it out, and my flesh was normal again, perfectly healed. This was God's way of saying, "I'm giving you power to deal with this situation," but still I was unsure. Who am I? I'm just a shepherd, an outcast, a murderer, and an adopted son of Egypt. I don't even know my real family.

My next strategy didn't go over so well either. I tried explaining to the Angel of the Lord that I was unqualified to speak and that my speech wasn't eloquent enough to convince a whole country to let God's people go. I said, "Lord, I'm slow of speech and I stumble over my words." His rebuking response was, "Who made man's mouth? Who makes him mute, or deaf, or seeing, or blind? Is it not I, the Lord? Now, go, and I will be with your mouth and teach you what you shall speak."

I pushed my luck once more and said, "Oh, my Lord, please send someone else." It became quite obvious that He was not happy with me. The anger of the Lord was kindled against me and He said, "Is there not Aaron, your brother, the Levite? I know that he can speak well. Behold, he is coming out to meet you, and when he sees you, he will be glad in his heart. You shall speak to him and put the words in his mouth, and I will be with your mouth and with his mouth and teach both of you what to do. He shall speak for you to the people, and he shall be your mouth, and you shall be as God to him. And take in your hand this staff, with which you shall do the signs."

I left my meeting with God having moved forward from my past; I was a humbled and changed man no longer wandering without purpose.

I AM LIKE MOSES

I am a reluctant misfit, a man culpable of committing murder, weary of running scared from past sins, and often guilty of downright rebellion in questioning God. My own heart deceives me and often I find it spiritually bankrupt. Yet just as God chose Moses, God chooses to use me, and for that I am grateful.

When I examine the life of Moses, I see that there isn't a whole lot of his story that is relatable to my own life. For example, I have no idea what it means to be born a Hebrew slave and then be miraculously positioned to live among the ruling elite in Egypt. I haven't murdered a man or fled to the desert wilderness in fear for my life and then be asked to deliver slaves from one of the most powerful countries in the world. But even though my life is far from Moses' time and culture, I can still relate to this great but weak biblical leader. I can place myself in his position, compare my own thoughts with his responses and apply them to my life.

Our stories may be different but our calling is the same. Sin, fear, and doubt often ruled Moses, but they have the same crippling effect on me. Regardless, our calling to trust is the same as what God asked Moses to do. Today God asks us to free people from the shackles of sin by offering the saving message of Jesus Christ, and we don't have to hike to the desert to fulfill our mission.

Moses was insecure, believing he was unqualified to do as God asked. He was probably asking himself why God would use a shepherd, a murderer, an outcast, and an adopted son of Egypt to save the Israelites from bondage. But God in His sovereignty knew exactly who would be the best candidate for the job. God allowed Moses' position in life to shape him for future ministry.

Unfortunately, Moses didn't try to understand how his life experiences were shaping him for this future role. God's positioning through his adoption into the royal family was extremely vital in that it gave him unparalleled access and respect that no other Hebrew had. His sense of justice, although he took it too far in killing the taskmaster, would serve him well in being tough enough to stand up to Pharaoh and see the slaves freed. His time leading and shepherding animals in the wilderness gave him skills, experience, and a great understanding of how to lead the Israelites with a firm but loving hand. Moses may not have felt qualified, but he was the perfect man for the job.

Throughout the Bible God demonstrates that He does not use

only perfect people to accomplish His plans. Biblical examples like Moses and others reinforce the theme that God often uses the weak and reluctant to do great things for Him. A perfect example of this is stated in 1 Corinthians 1:26–30:

> *For consider your calling, brothers: not many of you were wise according to worldly standards, not many were powerful, not many were of noble birth. But God chose what is foolish in the world to shame the wise; God chose what is weak in the world to shame the strong; God chose what is low and despised in the world, even things that are not, to bring to nothing things that are, so that no human being might boast in the presence of God. He is the source of your life in Christ Jesus, whom God made our wisdom and our righteousness and sanctification and redemption.*

THE STORY OF BILL BRONKEMA

Bill was a country boy who worked in a local supermarket. He went to church but wasn't a true believer. When asked if he was a Christian, he said yes, thinking that he was just as good as anyone else. Bill didn't drink, smoke, or swear as much as some people who called themselves believers, so he figured that made him a Christian.

When Bill was nineteen, his older brother invited him to attend a little mission church just outside of Grand Rapids, Michigan. The pastor of the church was working his way through the book of Romans and God used a couple of verses to really speak to Bill's heart. Romans 6:23 made him aware of his spiritual plight, "For the wages of sin is death, but the free gift of God is eternal life in Christ Jesus our Lord." Bill invited Jesus Christ into his heart as Lord and Savior of his life.

A few weeks later Bill's pastor spoke on Romans 10:14, "But how are they to call on him in whom they have not believed? And how are they to believe in him of whom they have never heard? And how are they to hear without someone preaching?" God used this verse to call Bill into full-time pastoral ministry.

Bill felt unqualified and inadequate, but he answered his ministry calling and went on to serve five years as pastor of a little country church and thirty years as the senior pastor at a Baptist church in Ortonville, Michigan. He retired from the pastorate to go to the mission field and served God for another ten years. Today Bill still serves in his local Florida church.

Bill would say that he isn't anybody special, but God used his gifts, and the impact of his ministry can still be felt to this day through the service of men who either grew up under his tutelage or worked under his leadership. Many are now serving God in pastoral or chaplain ministries.

A country boy was used by God to serve people for over forty years. As a young man his communication skills were raw and his English was bad. The first time he spoke to a group of youth, he covered the whole Bible twice and finished his entire message in about five minutes. It wasn't a great start, but over time God developed his skills to become an effective communicator. His story has similarities to that of Moses.

> *If God is calling you—go for it! He will supply your needs and will help you to grow in your faith*
> *—Reverend Bill D. Bronkema.*

A man may be running from past sins, questioning everything God is doing in his life or feeling unqualified to serve God. But God is in the business of using weak men who have sinned, fallen short, and on the surface may not be the most qualified. In fact, it is often the weak and reluctant whom God embraces and molds into the men He will ultimately use for His honor and glory.

> *All God's giants have been weak men who did great things for God because they reckoned on His being with them — James Hudson Taylor.*

> *Then the LORD said to him, 'Who has made man's mouth? Who makes him mute, or deaf, or seeing, or blind? Is it not I, the LORD? Now therefore go, and I will be with your mouth and teach you what you shall speak'* (Exodus 4:11–12).

Moses — Areas of weakness	How God used Moses
· Killed a man · Ran away · Felt unqualified · Felt unworthy · Questioned God · In the wilderness he tried to do things on his own and even got angry	· To free the Israelites from years of Egyptian bondage and slavery · To perform miracles · To bring the Ten Commandments to the people · To lead the Israelite nation through the wilderness for forty years · To provide them protection and provision

LIFE APPLICATION QUESTIONS:

(Read Exodus 1–14 for the whole Moses story.)

1. List all the excuses Moses brought before God at the burning bush when God called him to free the Israelites from slavery.
2. List all the ways that God reassured Moses that He would be with him.

> *We tend to make excuses when we allow our own insecurities to drive our decision-making process instead of trusting God even when He shows us that He has our back.*

3. Has God asked you to do something for Him?
4. What has been your response?
5. What does questioning God really say about the depth of someone's faith?
6. Did Moses' lack of qualifications prevent God from using him?

IF GOD USED MOSES IN SUCH A BIG WAY, THEN WHY NOT YOU?

Chapter Two

RUSTIC

Word was starting to get around. I wasn't sure how much time I would have to make a decision before the crowds gathered and wanted blood for her sin. I was a mental wreck. Negative emotions were swirling inside my head trying to sway my decision one way or the other, but my heart was leaning in one particular direction because I was in love with this woman. I knew I had a decision to make. I could either put her to public shame or I could divorce her quietly. Either way the result was going to break my heart. But there was no way that I would allow Mary to be harmed. I wasn't angry, just extremely disappointed.

It had been a whirlwind of a day and the tension of it all had worn me out. Surprisingly, I quickly fell asleep. A short time later I awoke to a minor body twitch and the realization that I had just experienced the most realistic dream of my life. Dreams weren't uncommon, but this dream was different. I couldn't sleep the rest of the night.

An angel of the Lord came to me and proclaimed, "Joseph, son of David, do not fear to take Mary as your wife, for that which is conceived in her is from the Holy Spirit. She will bear a son, and you shall call his name Jesus, for he will save his people from their sins." I pondered the words of the angel and what it all meant, all the while waiting for the sun to rise so I could run over to Mary and tell her of my decision to stick by her side. The sun couldn't come up fast enough.

Several months later when Mary was in the final stages of her pregnancy, we received word that Caesar Augustus had just decreed that all of the world should be registered. We would have to be registered in my home town, so we began to make preparations for our week-long journey to Bethlehem through winding mountains and dusty trails. It wouldn't be easy for a pregnant woman, but we had no choice. I trusted God's provision, especially since my wife was carrying God's Son.

I'm not sure why God chose me to be a part of this. I'm just a carpenter, an average man, not great at any one thing and often insecure about my own ability. Would I even be able to care for God's Son in a way that would honor Him? I continued on with my preparations for the trip but was distracted by the thoughts that this divine revelation had kicked off inside my head. Again my thoughts went back to why God chose me. I probably will never figure out the answer, but I suspect He chose Mary for the same reasons that captured my heart.

When we finally arrived in Bethlehem, I approached the town's inn. The door was shut and the lights were out, but there had to be someone home. I banged on the door but there was no answer. It was late in the evening because difficulties during our travels had caused us to arrive later than we had anticipated. We didn't have time to set up camp for the night. Besides, Mary's water had broken and we needed to get inside somewhere; God's baby was coming, and soon! I banged as loud as I could, but still nothing. I turned to walk away when the door opened and the voice of a gruff man bellowed, "You'll have to go somewhere else. There is no room for you here at this inn." I spun around and in a panicky voice declared, "But, my wife's pregnant! We need a place to stay. She is going to have this baby real soon."

"Go away and find somewhere else." The door slammed shut. What could we do now? Carefully, but in a hurry, we moved down the road. God would provide; I knew He would. I continued to say that in my head. A half mile down the dusty road Mary's contractions were getting worse and much closer together. It wouldn't be long now, so I prayed to God to provide us a place to stay.

The donkey was getting uncomfortable for Mary to ride, but her discomfort and pain wouldn't be any better if she tried to walk. Time was running out and we had no options. We struggled to reach the top of a hill knowing we had to press on. The clouds cleared revealing some light from the moon. It was enough to see a stable built into the side of the hill with animals occupying it. "We stop here," I told Mary. I moved some of the animals out of the way and found a nice soft place in the hay for Mary to deliver her baby.

Her contractions continued and I made preparations for Jesus to be born. I sure wished there had been a midwife there. I prayed again, "God give me the strength and wisdom to help deliver this baby." Everything was as good as it could be considering the circumstances, and an hour later the baby Jesus was born. I wrapped him in some swaddling cloths that we had brought just for this occasion. I gently handed Him back to Mary to hold, while I cleaned out the manger and placed some clean hay in the bottom of it so Jesus would have a place to rest when we weren't taking turns holding Him.

What happened next was almost indescribable. A bright star

shone down around us! Angels were rejoicing, then shepherds came to visit us praising God and worshiping our baby. It was an amazing night of celebration. I could tell that Mary was storing up all of this in her heart. It was a proud moment for her to be the mother of the Savior of the world.

Eight days went by and the Christ child was circumcised and officially named Jesus. It was another blessed day celebrating His miracle birth. Night couldn't come soon enough as we hadn't been getting much sleep because of all the visitors, celebrations, and attending to the baby in the middle of the night. At the end of a long day, I fell fast asleep as it was Mary's time to tend to the baby.

I would have another dream, but this time it wasn't the angel of the Lord bringing glad tidings of great joy. This time the message was dark, dangerous, and filled with peril. The Christ child was in danger, and this message brought news of death if we didn't flee immediately. The angel of the Lord said, "Rise, take the child and his mother, and flee to Egypt, and remain there until I tell you, for Herod is about to search for the child, to destroy him."

Immediately I awoke and packed up our things. In the middle of the night we fled. Our trip to Egypt would not be easy, but at this point we were just thankful for God's provision and protection. We would have to stay in Egypt until the time of Herod's death.

I would have another dream...

I AM LIKE JOSEPH.

I'm an average, ordinary man determined to get through life the best I can with minimal disruption and difficulties and doing my best to treat others as I would like to be treated. I like my life and its comforts, but often I find myself out of my comfort zone and right in the middle of God's plan.

In 2003, I answered God's call to leave the corporate world and enter into full-time ministry, starting an outdoor adventure ministry. From there God has worked in my heart and continues to transform me into the man He intends me to be. I'm still not there, but I'm working at it. Also, this process hasn't been without its fair share of fear, doubt, insecurities, and spiritual struggles; nonetheless, God has been patient, longsuffering, and good to me.

Over these past years, God has positioned me in Christian leadership and has developed me as a writer, public speaker, and chaplain. In addition, He has arranged for my ordination and my acquiring a master's degree in theological studies from Liberty University. I don't say that to brag but to show evidence of how God has been moving in the life of an average man. God continues to open doors of ministry to me that often don't make sense to others or even to me. There are times when I easily step out in faith and other times when I move forward hesitantly. Although the calling on my life is becoming clearer the older I become, it hasn't always been clear.

My story really begins with the bravery and courage of my grandfather who left all that he knew in the Netherlands and brought his young family to America. He couldn't speak English; he didn't have a job and had only $100 to his name. My mother was ten years old, a foreigner in a new land and an outcast on the playground at school because she talked funny. Near the end of her high school years she met a young man who liked to drag race cars. He came from an automotive family with little higher education. Her beauty caught his attention and they would eventually marry and raise three children in the small rural town of Ortonville, Michigan.

There was nothing exceptional about my childhood other than being part of a great family who loved God and enjoyed life. We went to church on a regular basis and loved the outdoors, especially hunting, fishing, and camping. As the middle child, I had to find ways to get the attention I needed. I was good at it as long as I was in the comfortable surroundings of my family.

However, in school I was quiet, shy, and laid-back. I was an average student, and during my high school years more than one teacher told me what my limitations were going to be. An English teacher told me that I would never be a professional writer, and a speech teacher proclaimed that I would never be a public speaker; I won't even mention what my math teacher thought about my algebra skills.

These weren't the most encouraging words to hear, but in fairness to my teachers, I hadn't really given them reason to think differently. My English and writing skills were terrible, and I didn't particularly pay close attention to what they were teaching me in class. I turned red whenever a girl mentioned my name, and being that shy was also a weakness in speech class. This made all of my attempts at public speaking very memorable, but for all the wrong reasons.

However there was always one area where I felt confident, and that was on a baseball field. Yet even in a sport I excelled in, my coach told me I would never be a great leader if I didn't find a way to become more vocal as the team captain. All of these accusations were not meant to be mean-spirited, but they reflected the reality of who I was at the time. Nevertheless, in ministry God chose to use my three biggest areas of weakness for His purposes.

I was the first person in my immediate family to get a bachelor's degree after six and a half years of working and going to school part-time. The one great accomplishment from this chapter in my life was that I came out with only a $1,300 college debt; on the other hand, my grades were just lackluster. I worked in the corporate world for nearly eight years where God blessed me financially, but I never really felt like that's where I belonged.

In 2003, I stepped out in faith, starting H2O adventure ministry, and began an amazing journey. All of my ministry accomplishments since then haven't happened because I am extremely gifted; rather, it was because I was willing to be stretched by God, leave my comfort zone, and be used in full-time ministry. It was very helpful having a loving and supportive wife. She has been an invaluable helpmate and encouragement to me during my ministry journey, even when it didn't make sense to the rest of the world.

I'm not special; in fact, I'm remarkably ordinary. I'm just a simple man from a small town whose soul is full of fears, doubts, and insecurities. I'm a man of humble beginnings and the child of an immigrant. I'm learning to trust God and experience the greatness of His love, even while sometimes battling Him along the way.

OUR BEGINNINGS SHAPE OUR FUTURES

When I think of all the great men and women mentioned in the Bible, my first thought is always amazement over what they were able to accomplish while coming from such humble beginnings. The most prominent example came from the life of Jesus Christ, who as God's Son was born of a virgin named Mary. She gave birth to Jesus in a stable because there was no room for them anywhere else. Our Savior was born in a place that resembled either a barn or a cave fit only for animals. It was definitely the humblest of beginnings.

There is spiritual growth that takes place when we are content knowing that one day our humble beginnings will help shape our future. When we successfully merge our past with the present workings of God, that is when our future ministry is fulfilled and we become the person God intended us to be.

The life of Christ was a life of humble simplicity, yet how infinitely exalted was his mission. Christ is our example in all things" —E.G. White.

Humble yourselves before the Lord, and He will exalt you" (James 4:10).

Joseph—Areas of weakness	How God used Joseph
· He was just an average man · He was a carpenter · Not a lot is known about him	· He married the mother of Jesus under unusual circumstances · He was the stepfather to God's Son and helped to rear Jesus · He was Mary's protector · God spoke to Joseph through dreams

LIFE APPLICATION QUESTIONS:

(Read Matthew 1 and 2 and Luke 2 for more on the birth of Jesus.)

1. Joseph received some news that would change his life abruptly. What was it, and what honorable points can you list that show how Joseph handled that news?
2. How did God reassure Joseph?

> *Positioning yourself within God's will is more important than working to position yourself within the world of men.*

3. When God asked Joseph to stick with Mary, it opened the way for criticism from his fellow man. If God asked you to do something that didn't make any sense to others, would you still do it?
4. The Scriptures don't say much about the life of Joseph, but it is safe to say that he was a man of humble beginnings. Did his position in life have any bearing on God choosing him?
5. In your own words, why do you think God chooses simple people to do His work or to be a part of His grand plans?

DON'T LET YOUR STATUS IN LIFE DICTATE HOW GOD CAN USE YOU!

Chapter Three

RAMPAGE

The door was easy to kick in. Nothing was going to stand in my way of dragging those heretics out of their homes to face the punishment they deserved. Screams from family members filled the room as my men physically assaulted the man of the house, grabbing him by the arms and neck and dragging him into the muddy street. The matriarch of the family tried to confront me as if she was going to do something about it, but I just gave her a look that helped her understand that I wasn't someone to mess with.

Righteous anger had been boiling inside me ever since the day when I realized that a segment of our people were a serious threat to our faith. It all began when I held the clothing of the men who executed Stephen, a false teacher and a prominent member of the Way, a small but growing group of people who follow the teachings of a dead Jesus, proclaiming that He is above all things, has risen from the dead and is our Messiah. The vicious attack might have crossed the line, but when Stephen spread his arms out in worship even as the rocks began flying and looked toward heaven and proclaimed, "Behold, I see the heavens opened, and the Son of Man standing at the right hand of God," I knew those followers of Jesus had to pay for their blasphemous ways. I'd do whatever it took to bring them all to justice.

This Jesus had the audacity to preach to us about our forefathers rejecting the Holy Spirit, Moses, and the prophets, and then telling us that we were doing the same thing. He went on to tell us that we had betrayed and murdered the Righteous One whom God had sent to deliver us. While I'm alive, this kind of heresy will not stand.

If anyone can boast about spiritual things, it would be me. I am a Pharisee, highly educated in the Scriptures and growing in rank, power, and wealth. I'm a Hebrew of all Hebrews. My ancestral lineage can be traced back to Jacob. I'm from the tribe of Benjamin and my zeal for God will not allow our faith to be trashed by some Jesus followers.

That wasn't the first time that Stephen and I had met. A few days before we stoned him, I challenged him to a debate about the Messiah. But it didn't go as well as I had planned. My talking points were correct and, as a group, my fellow Pharisees and I had every angle covered. But there was something different about Stephen. His points hit hard, yet they were amazingly full of grace. It was a strange experience. Every time we felt we had the upper hand, his arguments found a way to make our points seem weak. Without saying so, he was making us look like fools.

I was pleased to see Stephen put to death, and that was just the beginning. It was no time to be passive; it was time to act. My plan was to eradicate all of those who felt the need to undermine the traditional values of Judaism. My actions would be fully implemented even if I had to break down the door of every believers' gathering in the area. They could either flee which some did, or they could stand and face my fury.

So many did flee Judea to try and avoid my religious rampage that I approached the High Priest, Caiaphas, to ask for permission to pursue those fugitives all the way to Damascus. I would need official letters for each of the synagogues in order to put pressure on them to help root out those men and women of corruption.

The road to Damascus is more than one hundred and thirty miles long. Our journey would take more than a week to walk, and it would be challenging; but the goal was well worth all the dust and blisters. I was okay with the blisters as they would eventually become calloused and make my feet tougher, fitting for how I was feeling toward those Jesus followers. Maybe I'd ride a horse, but either way it wouldn't matter because after I rounded them all up, I'd bind them with whatever could be found and bring every one of them back to Jerusalem to face trial and, most likely, execution.

Nearing Damascus, our excitement picked up as we were that much closer to getting rid of these opponents of God and protecting our faith. Suddenly, a flash of light exploded around me with a supernatural brilliance. Its impact threw me to the ground. Immediately I knew that I was in the presence of something higher and more powerful than myself. A thundering voice called out my name, "Saul, Saul, why are you persecuting me?" My body trembled as those words echoed to the depths of my soul. I was unable to formulate any thoughts, much less figure out what to say; then, to my surprise, I responded, "Who are you, Lord?"

His reply was authoritative, kingly in a majestic sort of way: "I am Jesus, whom you are persecuting." It was like a punch to the gut hearing Him speak those words. The men with me stood speechless. They could hear the booming voice but could not see the person who had brought me to my knees. He continued, "But rise and enter the city, and you will be told what you are to do."

I lay on the ground trembling and soaking in the first part of His statement, "I am Jesus, whom you are persecuting." Those words reached to my inner core; I was overcome with indescribable emotion. My life's foundation was shattered. Somebody grabbed me by the arms and pulled me to my feet. Blinded by this encounter with God, I began to blink, rub and lift my eyelids in hopes of regaining my sight, but it was no use. Under normal circumstances, crying out at the revelation of losing one's eye sight would be considered normal, but Jesus' words stayed in my heart rendering me hours of silent reflection. The men brought me to Damascus, and for three days I couldn't eat or drink. Earthly sustenance was the last thing on my mind; entering into a personal relationship with Jesus was all I could think about.

Then a man entered the room where I was and laid his hands over my eyes. He proclaimed, "Brother Saul, the Lord Jesus who appeared to you on the road by which you came has sent me so that you may regain your sight and be filled with the Holy Spirit." As his words came out of his mouth, scales from my eyes fell to the ground; I could see clearly now. They gave me food to strengthen my weakened body, but I wouldn't eat any of it until after I was baptized.

I spent the next few days in Damascus with the disciples of Jesus, gaining strength and confounding the Jews and myself as I spoke the name of Jesus in the local synagogues. I continued on until the Jews began to plot against me in the same and wicked way that I had done to my brother in Christ, Stephen, and so many other innocent martyrs after him.

Catching wind of their plot to kill me, and with the help of the disciples, I hid. The gates were being watched day and night. There would be no chance of escape through the gates of the city. I would have to go either under the wall or over it, but it was a long way down. One of my Christian brothers who only days before would have been on my execution list was now helping me plot my escape.

His plan was to lower me in a basket at a place where he knew there was a hole in the wall. This would make it easier to lower someone to safety. We waited for nightfall before executing my getaway.

My new friends called me Paul; I was a new creation in Christ, working hard to press on toward the upward call of God, forgetting what lay behind me and allowing the old man to fade. Thankful for the collision with Jesus on the road to Damascus, I was changed forever. Although I yearn to be in heaven, I recognize that there is still work to be done here on earth, and it comes with the understanding that it won't come without a price.

I AM LIKE SAUL.

Saul was an educated man filled with knowledge of the Scriptures yet often interfering with the workings of God in the name of ardent spirituality. Like Saul, I deal with a life of past sin, answering the call to ministry, learning to put the past behind me, fighting the reliance on a resumé, struggling to put aside the legalistic aspects of my faith, while endeavoring every day to become more Christlike.

The apostle Paul is a great example to me of a person who, when touched by the power of Christ, became a new man. One way he was able to demonstrate that change was by leaving his name, Saul, which was associated with all of the Christian persecution he was involved in, and becoming known as Paul, a new man in Christ.

Often, in my own life I look back on my past failures and believe they disqualify me from future ministry. But that is a lie as long as the sin has been properly dealt with. A belief in this kind of falsehood puts me in a position of questioning whether God's Word is true and also minimizes what Christ did for me on the cross. So, if my past disqualifies me from being used by God, then why does He use imperfect people like Paul and me?

God has a plan for my life. Yes, sin is a part of my world and that will never change, but sin doesn't exclude me from being used by God unless I am unwilling to deal with it and put it behind me.

SPIRITUAL AMBITIONS

When my son was a cute two-year old, his ambition in life was to go to the beach and eat sand all day long. When he turned into a rambunctious three-year-old, his interests changed and he stopped eating sand. Instead, he resorted to dipping his head in the toilet and from there morphed into challenging himself in various ways around the house, usually at our expense.

One day I came home from work to what sounded like a faucet running upstairs. I went to investigate and caught my son standing at the top of the stairs, seeing how many steps he could reach as he relieved himself. His grin was from ear to ear, and his squeaky voice said, "Daddy, I set a record." I found it quite laughable until I realized that a record implies having done it at least once before.

When we are young in our faith, our spiritual ambitions are somewhat immature and often lack depth; but as we grow in our relationship with God, He changes our holy interests into something much greater. My son is older now, and his interests are changing in a positive way; there has even been talk of future ministry, but as for now he is open to God's leading in his life, and it's not time yet for him to make those big decisions.

C.S. Lewis has a great quote that speaks to our willingness to settle for less when God has so much more for us. He said,

> *Indeed if we consider the unblushing promise of reward and the staggering nature of the rewards promised in the Gospels, it would seem that our*

> *Lord finds our desires not too strong, but too weak. We are half-hearted creatures like an ignorant child who wants to go on making mud-pies in a slum because he cannot imagine what is meant by the offer of a holiday at the sea. We are too easily pleased.*

Too often I am content with being stuck in the mud instead of enjoying the riches of God's love, provision, and protection. The enemy tries to convince me that the mud-pie is the better option, but that's also a lie. God wants me to seek His forgiveness, forget what lies behind and press forward, cultivating a more intimate relationship with Him. When I do this, my ambitions change.

SAUL THE OVERCOMER

Saul, who became known as Paul, overcame a painful past to go on to do great things for God. But what makes his story so remarkable is what he did to improve his spiritual ambitions. In Paul's letter to the Philippians, he wrote about how he was not perfect but continued to press forward, straining for the upward call of God in Christ Jesus. He understood that even though he was doing great things for God, he had not totally arrived at his spiritual destination. He knew that he had not received everything or become everything, nor had Paul done everything that God was calling him to do.

Paul believed in honest introspection. He knew who he was from the inside out and from the bad to the good. Paul recognized his strengths and weaknesses, but ultimately knew that his power came from the Lord. If anyone could brag about their stature it was the Apostle Paul. He had a great religious resumé. He was a Pharisee and was circumcised in the Hebrew faith as the custom was back then. His family lineage went through the tribe of Benjamin and could be traced all the way back to Abraham. Paul was a Hebrew among Hebrews. He strictly followed the law and even considered himself to be blameless. He had a righteous zeal and was also a persecutor of Christians. Paul knew that he must forget his past sins and the deep-rooted legalisms that were such a part of his faith.

Paul's past was filled with misguided religious turbulence and spiritual accolades that were now being set aside for a present and future life of meaningful ministry. Paul learned to reject his own righteousness and considered his own gains as mere rubbish. Paul was now a true follower of Jesus, resting everything on the strength and power of Jesus Christ.

This was an amazing transformation for a man who was once all about himself. Now his goal was to decrease so that Christ might increase. Saul, a weak man, humbled by the revealing of his own sin nature, would go on to become Paul, a weak man, who would have a tremendous impact teaching others about the love and peace of Jesus, influencing others to recognize the saving grace of God.

Paul knew his work here on earth wasn't done and that he would always need the daily process of sanctification to work in his life. Paul's example of dealing with his past and putting it behind him and then allowing his weak nature to be used by God is ever an encouragement to me.

> *A man can no more diminish God's glory by refusing to worship Him than a lunatic can put out the sun by scribbling the word, darkness on the walls of his cell —C.S. Lewis.*

> *Do not be conformed to this world, but be transformed by the renewal of your mind, that by testing you may discern what is the will of God, what is good and acceptable and perfect* (*Romans 12:2*).

Saul—Areas of weakness	How God used Paul
· He participated in the stoning death of Stephen · He persecuted Christians · He was judgmental · He was pious · He had misguided zeal	· He brought the Gospel message to the Gentiles · He took three major missionary journeys · He planted churches and discipled Christians · He led people to Christ, including prisoners, royalty and many others · He authored thirteen books of the Bible · He encouraged generation upon generation of believers through his writings

LIFE APPLICATION QUESTIONS: *(Read Acts 6–9 for more of the story of Stephen and Saul.)*

1. What was Saul's motive in executing those early Christians?

2. Did Saul's past sins keep God from using Saul in the future?

Often our presuppositions, pride, and arrogant beliefs can influence our view of how God works. His ways are much higher than our ways. Saul thought he had God figured out, but he was on the wrong side in his zeal to do what he thought was right.

3. What character trait of Saul did God like and how did it benefit him as Paul?

DON'T MAKE IT YOUR ONLY GOAL TO INFLUENCE MAN; RATHER, LET GOD SHAPE YOUR ZEAL FOR HIM TO CHANGE YOU.

Chapter Four

PRISONER

The moss-covered walls were closing in around me; a claustrophobic reaction was only minutes away. The air was damp and cold; being waist deep in wet mud made for inhospitable living conditions. I had been down here too long; I needed to get out!

The noose around my chest tightened, making it difficult to breathe, and the rope cut into my flesh causing me to scream. My direction quickly reversed after my outburst and soon my feet were touching the ground again. Rags rained down on me and I did as I was instructed, putting the rags between the rope and my armpits. The tattered rags helped ease my pain a little, but my freedom would not come without scrapes, rope burns, and some oxygen deprivation. The deep and abandoned cistern acted as both a prison and a grave. Those who hated me had left me to die.

During my painful ascent, I reflected on the tribulations I'd encountered since that time as a teenager when God called me to be one of His prophets. What had followed was imprisonment, death threats, beatings, and being locked up in stocks. Spending a few days in a dark mud hole while leeches sucked the blood out of me were nothing compared to the ostracizing I received for speaking the words of God.

It has been close to forty years since that day when the Lord came to me saying, "Before I formed you in the womb I knew you, and before you were born I consecrated you; I appointed you a prophet to the nations."

It was an amazing encounter, but that wasn't enough to keep me from pointing out the obvious: I was only a youth and wasn't an eloquent speaker. The Lord, however, called me out and declared, "Do not say, 'I am only a youth'; for to all to whom I send you, you shall go, and whatever I command you, you shall speak. Do not be afraid of them, for I am with you to deliver you."

The Lord put out His hand. He touched my mouth and spoke the words, "Behold, I have put my words in your mouth. See, I have set you this day over nations and over kingdoms, to pluck up and to break down, to destroy and to overthrow, to build and to plant."

I saw an almond branch and a boiling pot facing away from the north. They meant that God was watching and disaster would be loosed out of the north. Various armies from the north would surround the gates of Jerusalem. The people would pay a price for forsaking God and worshiping other gods.

Over the years my adversaries have attempted to maim, kill, or harm me in many ways, but God's protection has always undermined their heinous plots. I'll never forget when the Lord told me to arise and to be prepared for my coming work and to not be afraid of saying everything that He commanded me to say. His words give me comfort every time I'm faced with a painful hardship. He said, "And I, behold, I make you this day a fortified city, an iron pillar, and bronze walls, against the whole land, against the kings of Judah, its officials, its priests, and the people of the land. They will fight against you, but they shall not prevail against you, declares the LORD, for I am with you, to deliver you."

I AM LIKE JEREMIAH

I'm inexperienced and not a super-dynamic speaker. Yet God doesn't seem to care about any of that. In spite of it all, He chooses to use me by positioning me to be able to encourage and reveal God to others.

Sometimes God calls me to do things that I never would have signed up for. In my case it was being a Christian speaker. I wasn't going to raise my hand and volunteer. It was so outside of who I thought I was, but God knew best and the following story is how God drafted me into the ministry of His choosing.

On a cool, crisp, and clear November afternoon, the conditions for bagging a big whitetail deer were perfect. It was the peak of rutting season with virtually no breeze, and half-a-dozen doe were already spilling into the surrounding woods. A hunter couldn't ask for better circumstances.

All of the doe quickly snapped to attention, and that is when I knew it was time. An eight-pointer sauntered into view. There was no need for an introduction; he was the "king of the woods." Focused and obsessed with his trophy rack, my first thought was how I was going to convince my wife that this deer's head would look great over our bed. My wife, Sarah, is a pretty fair and flexible woman, so she gave me some options. She said, "You can hang it out in the garage, down in the basement, or—if it really means that much to you—you can hang it over the bed in your new apartment."

The buck jumped when my arrow hit the ground just in front of him. Still unaware of where the sudden thud came from, the eight-pointer intent on finding an estrous doe pressed on. Armed with only two arrows, my next shot had to be on target.

The last arrow in the quiver took flight and sailed over the back of that eight-point buck. In almost a mocking gesture, the mighty buck raised his shoulders and lifted his head high as he casually worked his way toward a nearby grazing doe. Then, no longer armed, I sat helpless, and watched him saunter to the other side of the woods, eventually moving out of sight.

I was so focused on his mighty rack that I was willing to do just about anything for a third chance. I climbed down from my tree stand and, with the stealth of a rhino, I was able to reach my first arrow, presently stuck in the mud. Sitting on both knees, I yanked it out and was able to clean the broad head as I saw that familiar flash of white coming back in my direction. There was still hope.

A thirty-yard broadside shot presented itself in just a matter of seconds. The arrow, back in flight again, raced toward the unsuspecting buck. The impact of the arrow ripped through the flesh of a little sapling tree before it stopped. To my dismay, there I sat, lowly in the mud, watching the deer of my dreams walk off into the sunset.

It was a gloomy day a week later with forty-to-fifty-mile-an-hour winds howling through the woods. Gun season was drawing near and the cold air was piercing. Immediately upon reaching my tree stand, I caught a glimpse of a whitetail flag off in the distance. Did I scare off a new deer? No, it was the same eight-point buck after a doe.

In our earlier encounter, this whitetail trophy came out victorious, but I knew that this day would be different. I knew what had to be done. Years of training quickly came flooding back. My focus no longer rested on boasting or on the distraction of his big body and mighty rack; instead, my target became a matter of enjoying the hunt.

This time the giant deer took my ability for granted, taunting me by coming closer. I'm sure he thought he was safe since I had missed him three times the week before. The impact of the arrow sent a shockwave through his body. This day would be a day of victory.

It's not often that a whitetail deer, a happy taxidermist, and a misunderstood invitation would be the backdrop for a story about God doing the impossible. The details are still very clear and it seems just like yesterday that I was driving to Port Huron, Michigan, for my first-ever public speaking event. I had the radio down low so I could clearly hear the words coming out of my mouth saying that this wasn't going to be a big deal. After all, how hard could it be since I was supposed to give only a five-minute testimony?

After shooting that big eight-pointer I had called a taxidermist recommended to me by my brother-in-law. The taxidermist's name was Pat. When he answered the phone I could tell right away that he was a character in a good way, full of life and optimistic.

Our conversation began with some general introductions and then I told him that I had shot this whitetail buck and that I wanted the head to be mounted. But because I had just started a Christian outdoor adventure ministry, I didn't have the money to pay for it right then. I asked him if I could make small payments until the bill was paid in full.

Pat interrupted, "Tell me more about this outdoor ministry." So I explained to him what God had been doing in my life and how I felt the call to start an outdoor adventure ministry designed to motivate, encourage, and strengthen men to live for Christ. When I was done he said, "Mike, I want to mount that deer for you for free. All I ask is that you do something for me in return. Come to our church's wild-game dinner and give your testimony." I wondered how hard that could be, After all, my testimony was so boring it would take only five minutes. So I agreed to the deal and was excited to tell my wife about what had just transpired. Little did I know how God was going to use this conversation with a man whom I had never met before to change the course and direction of my spiritual journey.

On the drive over to Port Huron, I convinced myself that I'd be speaking at a small church and everyone in attendance would already be a Christian. There would be no need to share the Gospel message and all fifty of the congregation would be merciful as I clumsily spoke. My testimony about coming to Christ at a young age would easily resonate with all of them. All that changed the moment I pulled into the parking lot of a large contemporary church, and so would the rest of my misguided expectations about what this night would hold.

An exuberant Pat met me at the door and handed me the events program. I quickly glanced through the night's activities to see where I would be speaking. To my surprise, I located my name in the keynote speaker's slot. I looked up at Pat in shock and he just looked at me and grinned. After my mind cleared from the shock I asked him if he thought most of the 300 to 400 people in attendance were believers. He responded that actually eighty percent were unsaved people from the local community. Not only was I now the keynote speaker, but I would also need to quickly include the Gospel message. I had nothing prepared.

To make matters worse, the dinner went long. A Department of Natural Resources speaker was dry and boring and the church's prize drawings took over a half hour to complete. Once the last prize was drawn I could hear every chair in the room scoot backwards. It was time for all of them to get out of there. The M.C. quickly ran up on the platform and told the crowd that they had one more speaker to go. I could hear the crowd sigh in unison.

Not only was I not prepared to be the keynote speaker, now I had to face a crowd that wanted to be somewhere else. I was faced with having to speak to this crowd. I prayed and made some jokes about having the same name as the boxer, Mike Tyson, which loosened up the crowd and helped them settle down. I began to tell the story of how it took me four shots to get my big buck, even though I had only two arrows in my quiver. The Holy Spirit helped me with bringing out some spiritual truths and to formulate the words for a Gospel message. I was hooked and my Christian speaking ministry was born.

> *The flower of youth never appears more beautiful than when it bends toward the sun of righteousness—Matthew Henry.*

> *The heart of man plans his way, but the LORD establishes his steps (Proverbs 16:9).*

Jeremiah—Areas of weakness	How God used Jeremiah
· He was only a youth when called · He was not an eloquent speaker	· He became a major prophet of God · He proclaimed God's word · He declared judgment and doom · He was persecuted for being a prophet of God

LIFE APPLICATION QUESTIONS:

(Read the book of Jeremiah for more of the story, but read Jeremiah 1 to answer these questions.)

1. What were Jeremiah's reasons for not feeling qualified to serve God?

2. What was God's response?

> *When God calls you to serve, youth or inexperience are not viable excuses. God will not allow others to prevail over you if He has called you to do something for Him.*

3. What type of persecution did Jeremiah face?

4. God did not promise Jeremiah that he wouldn't experience persecution; but what did God promise would happen to those who sought Jeremiah's destruction?

DON'T LET YOUR YOUTH BE AN EXCUSE
TO NOT ENGAGE IN MINISTRY.
IF GOD HAS CALLED YOU, YOU ARE QUALIFIED.

Chapter Five

RECKLESS

It had been a long day, but a day filled with miracles and blessing. Our Teacher told us to get into the boat, so all twelve of us crammed into the fishing boat that wasn't necessarily designed for twelve fishermen. Luckily for all of us, we were in pretty good shape from all of the walking we had done with the Master since our time with Him began. We assumed our trip to the other side of the sea would be uneventful; I needed some rest.

The first part of our luxury cruise, as one disciple joked, went pretty well, but then the waves began to build and a strong wind seemed to come out of nowhere. Waves crashed over the bow, and we had trouble holding on. We were tossed into each other like rag dolls; it was funny the first couple of times, but now it was getting serious.

All of us had made a commitment to be a part of something bigger than ourselves and we knew there would be some sacrifices to be made along the way; drowning at sea wasn't one of them. Wave after wave crashed into the boat, nearly swamping it. The winds picked up more strength and we began to cower in the bottom of the boat. Men familiar with the ways of the sea, were now trapped by fear. It was getting bad.

Just as we were losing all hope, something strange happened. We saw a man coming in our direction walking on the water. It was late, well into the fourth watch of the night, and some of us thought we were seeing a ghost. I wondered, is this what happens just before you die? Some of the men cried out in fear and that is when we heard a familiar voice, "Take heart; it is I. Do not be afraid." I knew that voice.

In my time with the Master, I had not always been one to sit back and wait. I tend to be impulsive and often try to force things to happen; I jump before thinking. The Master had a lot of patience with me. I'm working at patience, but sometimes I rely on my own strength to accomplish what needs to be done. This time was no different.

It was hard to hear with that strong wind blowing, but I knew that voice and so I yelled as loud as I could, "Lord, if it is you, command me to come to you on the water." He replied, "Come." So to the surprise of the others I jumped out of the boat and began to run toward Jesus. He was grinning from ear to ear, much the same way as a father watching his child walk for the first time.

My run slowed to a walk. My attention shifted off Jesus and to the waves rolling all around me. Doubt crept in; then the wind began to swirl, spraying me with water and then my doubt turned to fear. I began to sink. I looked at Jesus and His grin had vanished, replaced by a look of mild disappointment. I cried out, "Lord, save me!" Immediately He reached out and took hold of my hand. He pulled me out of the sea and under His power we were able to walk on the water as we made our way to the boat. Jesus said to me, "O you of little faith, why did you doubt?"

The rest of the boat ride was calm, which gave me time to lean on James; he always made for a great pillow in cramped quarters and I spent the rest of the time in reflection about how we disciples have acted around Jesus. Not only do we try to do things in our own power, but we try to position ourselves in ministry for all the wrong reasons. A good example of this was that time when we were all sitting around talking with Jesus. James's and John's mother happened to be there and she asked Jesus something that made all of us cringe. She said, "Say that these two sons of mine are to sit, one at your right hand and one at your left, in your kingdom." Jesus replied, "You do not know what you are asking. Are you able to drink the cup that I am to drink?"

"We are able," they responded.

"You will drink my cup, but to sit at my right hand and at my left is not mine to grant, but it is for those for whom it has been prepared by my Father."

Shouts of disgust arose from the ranks of the disciples, but Jesus continued, "You know that rulers of the Gentiles lord it over them, and their great ones exercise authority over them. It shall not be so among you. But whoever would be great among you must be your servant, and whoever would be first among you must be your slave, even as the Son of Man came not to be served but to serve, and to give His life as a ransom for many."

That day we all learned that position and title mean very little in the kingdom of God; having a servant's heart is what matters most. The Master has loved us, yet He has been firm in what He has taught us. Serving others has been a central theme in His teachings, and it has only increased our faith.

Stepping out in faith has never been an issue for me, but waiting on God and resting in His power is what sometimes gets the best of me. I've done some good things, but I have also some epic failures to go along with them. There was the time when I fell asleep three times when Jesus had specifically asked us to stay awake and watch while He was troubled in the garden. And when the officials of the temple came to arrest Him, I cut off a man's ear. Jesus restored his ear. It was another teaching moment for me. To make matters worse, after His arrest, I denied being a follower of Christ, not once, but three times.

My time spent with Jesus definitely had its ups and downs, and often my zeal in serving Him got in the way of what He was really trying to teach us. Yet His love for us never ceased to amaze me. I remember one time when we were discussing what others thought about Jesus and who they thought He was. Jesus asked me a simple question: "But who do you say that I am?" I answered from the bottom of my heart, "You are the Christ, the Son of the living God." He was pleased and responded, "Blessed are you, Simon Bar-Jonah! For flesh and blood has not revealed this to you, but my Father who is in heaven. And I tell you, you are Peter, and on this rock I will build my church, and the gates of hell shall not prevail against it. I will give you the keys of the kingdom of heaven, and whatever you bind on earth shall be bound in heaven, and whatever you loose on earth shall be loosed in heaven." Then He said we should tell nobody at this time that He is the Christ. I was okay with that because I have found that His timing is always perfect.

I AM LIKE PETER.

I'm just like the man who at times was hasty, reckless, and in the beginning intent on doing things his own way. Position and title were often more important to him than actual ministry. I'm like Peter who denied Christ three times within a twenty-four-hour period. I think I too have denied the deity and power of Christ in my life, failing to surrender completely to Him on a daily basis.

I've noticed that in man's world, position is everything; but in God's universe position means absolutely nothing. We men constantly strive for better positions in all aspects of life, sacrificing what is important for the temporary to boost our finances or ego. Many of us have had our worlds collapse around us while chasing a better lifestyle, often leaving behind us a wake of destruction.

I've found that in amateur sports, for example, the bar keeps getting raised. It's no longer good enough just to make the team, be a supportive teammate, and have fun participating. Now, a player must be a starter, play on an elite travel team with long seasons and exorbitant player and equipment fees. The goal is no longer recreation but training with the expectation of becoming a professional athlete, even though the statistics are similar to that of winning the lottery.

I can see that politics has been greatly influenced by men and women who are more interested in keeping their political seat than voting in the best interests of their constituents. Political agendas too often override doing what is right for the country. Consequences are often ignored by the person seeking political position or title. The pursuit of power can consume a man's core values and morals, all in a quest to tell others what to do and to hold onto their own power.

Around me in the workplace, some men who seek a better pay grade, position, or title are willing to sacrifice time with their families by working long hours in hopes of achieving success. They will compromise their spiritual health to pursue advancement while neglecting family, physical health, and the things of God. They strive to reach the bar that continues to move and work at what will still be there tomorrow.

I earned a master's degree in theological studies from Liberty University and then went on to be ordained. People told me that

I was ready to be a pastor. I thought so too. My home church had confirmed that I was called to ministry. So I set out to find a pastoral position. I sent my resumé to numerous churches across the nation. The process seemed to be moving in the right direction. I was filling out doctrinal statements, answering questionnaires, and I was beginning to get some responses and some interviews. But even when I reached various levels of the interview process, even as far as preaching at a church, things just never seemed right.

Either I wasn't a good fit for their church or that church wasn't a good fit for me and my family. God was closing doors, but I continued to press on because that is what I was told to do and that is what I thought God wanted me to do. So I pressed forward, trying to find the perfect church. God closed more doors until I finally gave up and realized this wasn't happening right now.

I knew that I was called to ministry, but I thought that would be as a pastor. Later I came to the conclusion that the timing just wasn't right, but I was still searching for ministry opportunities. I began to search on the internet for information about being a chaplain. I loved sports and thought it would be a great idea to be a chaplain for a pro team or a college team. That is when God began the process of showing me what my heart longing was really about. I came across the chaplain page of Fellowship of Christian Athletes (F.C.A.) and sent an inquiry to them to find out how to become a chaplain.

I contacted them, and to make a long story short there was mutual interest in me becoming the F.C.A. Area Director for all of southeast Michigan. I spent close to a year working with F.C.A. while trying to raise financial support for this position. But God again closed the door. Frustration was beginning to mount as I was still convinced that I was supposed to be involved in ministry. Yet, at that time, I was no longer pursuing ministry of any kind.

I began to feel that maybe God wanted me to write and continue my speaking ministry, so I worked at being content in my situation. Then God started bringing me ministry offers that I wasn't even searching for. As I began pursuing those, the doors would close again for various reasons. It was a difficult couple of years for me while I tried to explain the direction of my life to others.

It became clear to me what God had been trying to teach me through these frustrating times. God showed me that I can pursue all of the ministry I want, but if He isn't in it, then those doors will be closed. Then He showed me that I was more concerned with getting a position or a title in order to please man than I was at being able to do ministry for Him. Then when God brought me those opportunities I wasn't even seeking, it was to show me that at any time He could bring me a ministry position and do it in His timing.

Since then I have learned to be content with where God puts me. I'm no longer concerned about pleasing man and trying to explain my life to others. Instead, I'm happy doing the unique ministries that God places before me. He has positioned me with a writing ministry, a speaking ministry, and the opportunity to be the team chaplain for the Detroit Thunder, a pro-indoor football team. God is good, and even when I don't understand everything that is going on, I've learned that I just need to trust Him. I've also learned to abide by the words of Colossians 3:23–24 which state, "Whatever you do, work heartily, as for the Lord and not for men, knowing that from the Lord you will receive the inheritance as your reward. You are serving the Lord Christ."

Not only do I have unique ministry opportunities because of where God has placed me, but I also am able to coach and spend quality time with my family.

I'm often like Peter, trying desperately to force the situation, but like him I've also learned to let God do His thing in His time and in His way. Fame, success, salary, position, or title is not what defines me; my relationship with Jesus Christ defines me. I'm not working to please men; I'm working to please my Creator.

> *Only God who made us can touch us and change us and save us from ourselves" —Billy Graham.*

> *Guard your steps when you go to the house of God. To draw near to listen is better than to offer the sacrifice of fools, for they do not know that they are doing evil. Be not rash with your mouth, nor let your heart be hasty to utter a word before God, for God is in heaven and you are on earth. Therefore let your words be few* (Ecclesiastes 5:1–2).

THE STORY OF DALLAS JENKINS

The son of best-selling author Jerry B. Jenkins, Dallas Jenkins is a man who spent ten years making good, quality, and moral family movies. After a while he felt his spiritual life was becoming a little dry. Dallas was a filmmaker living in Los Angeles with his eyes set on making movies outside of the "ministry bubble" and whose initial goal was to make full-length feature films that the world could appreciate. However, God had other plans.

He says that his resistance to authority and his assumption that he always knew what was best were his biggest weaknesses. But when he learned to get out of God's way and put aside his own ideas, his spiritual impact really took shape and his spiritual life no longer felt dry. God moved him from L.A. to the Chicago area to work with Harvest church in creating feature-length films. Dallas believes he has done his best work since working with a team in this new church context as opposed to working on his own. "It's been great to discover that I'm not as smart as I thought I was and that I'm ultimately in God's hands. Besides that I'm genuinely enjoying life more." As a result he ended up making hundreds more videos and two more short films than he had ever planned to make. Dallas, says, "They made me a better filmmaker." He hopes to exhibit this in his upcoming feature film, "The Resurrection of Gavin Stone."

Dallas's new short films have led numerous people into a personal relationship with Jesus Christ. He is humbled that God would use his work to reach others. Dallas says, "There's a big difference between happy and comfortable and joy. Joy is eternal, joy is big, and you don't get that unless you're passionately pursuing God's will." Now his mission is to change the conversation about Christ and the church's role in popular culture and to show people that grace is possible.

> *My passion and intensity have always been strengths, but now that they're in the right context, God has allowed my creative abilities to flourish"*
> *— Dallas Jenkins.*

Peter—Areas of weakness	How God used Peter
· He was reckless · He was hasty · He denied Christ three times · He chopped off a man's ear · He often tried to do things on his own	· To be the "Rock" of Christ's church · To witness many of Jesus' miracles · To walk on water—briefly · To preach to both Jews and Gentiles · To write the letters 1 and 2 Peter · To witness the Transfiguration · To be an influential leader of the early church

LIFE APPLICATION QUESTIONS:

(The stories of Peter can be read throughout the Gospels.)

1. List the different ways that Peter was hasty or reckless in his approach to ministry?
2. What were some of the consequences of Peter's actions?

> *Being hasty, reckless, or self-serving in ministry is not what God wants from us, and the results can lead to serious consequences for those who are under the care of our leadership.*

3. When Peter failed and denied Christ three times, what was Christ's response?
4. Peter's hasty actions and the consequences that followed were often the result of good intentions. Doing things his way usually resulted in being outside of what Christ was doing. In ministry have you ever done something hasty but with good intentions only to have what you did go bad? If so, have you made amends to those who were hurt as a result?

FAME, SUCCESS, POSITION, OR TITLE DOES NOT DEFINE A MAN. OUR RELATIONSHIP WITH JESUS CHRIST IS WHAT DEFINES EACH OF US!

Chapter Six

STORM

Night fog surrounded the boat; its presence was haunting. But the darkness and fog ignored their hard and difficult labor. The stench of their nets and their clothes betrayed their profession.

Galilee, a fishing community, was home to two brothers who sat defeated on the shore after a long night of failure and empty fishing nets. They were average men, living average lives. Little did they know that their lives were about to be changed forever when the Great Light of God would dawn upon them and illuminate their souls with the need to save the world.

It was a long night of fishing with nothing to show for it. As the night turned to dawn, the growing light revealed a man on the shore with a crowd of people following Him. This man looked familiar; they had seen Him before. He approached the fishermen, and without invitation, climbed into their boat. He asked them to put out a little from the shore and they did as He asked. Their fishing-boat guest stood up, faced the growing crowd on shore and began to teach.

When He had finished speaking, He said to one of the fishermen, "Put out into the deep water and let down your nets for a catch." One of them replied, "Master, we've worked hard all night and haven't caught anything. But because you say so, I will let down the nets."

The fishermen, familiar with the routine, began the process of lowering their nets. Immediately the boat shifted from the weight of the fish entangled in the nets. The fishermen were thrilled yet nervous at the same time. Neither had ever felt this kind of weight in the nets. The nets filled beyond their limits, and were stretching and popping as if they were about to tear in half. The burden the nets carried was starting to sink the boat. Reinforcements were needed, as the work was too much for them. They signaled to their fishing partners, James and John, to come over and help. The results for them were the same, and now they had two fishing boats about to capsize from the weight of the fish. The boats would just make it to shore.

The gravity of the situation sank in and the passionate one of the group, Peter, fell down at the Teacher's feet saying, "Depart from me for I am a sinful man, O Lord!"

The men had been seized with amazement because of the unbelievable catch of fish. The Teacher, understanding the situation, replied, "Do not fear! From now on you will be catching men."

Four men, Peter, Andrew, James, and John, heeded Christ's calling and left everything behind, including their profession and the security and comfort of their hometown. They knew Jesus was worth following, but did they truly understand the challenge of the adventure they were about to begin?

Tired fishermen, who hours before had experienced a sea filled with darkness, empty nets, and nothing to hope for, now experienced the miraculous and saving power of the Great Light. That morning, Jesus, the Light of the World, began the supernatural and spiritual transformation of four average men; He called them to an exciting experience and a bold undertaking. It would be the greatest adventure of their lives.

THE ADVENTURE BEGINS

Another wave crashed over their boat and all on board desperately grasped for anything to hold onto; there wasn't much. It wasn't that long ago when these men had made a heartfelt commitment to be a part of something bigger than themselves. Every day seemed to be a new adventure.

That day began like any other day; the sun rose out of the east and slowly moved overhead. The friends were ready for another day with the Teacher. They would follow Him anywhere. Each new day with the Teacher was never the same as the last, but maybe they could hope for a little familiarity to ease the stretching of their comfort zones. Regardless, it seemed like it would be another great day.

But huge waves now pounded the wooden fishing boat. Yes, the boat was designed to be out on the big waves of the sea, but this storm was different. It was bigger than any storm these men had experienced over the years. Those experienced fishermen wanted to be out of that boat—that's how bad it had gotten. They knew that if the storm continued it wouldn't be long before a big wave would scoop them right out of the boat and into the dangerous waters.

Shouts and screams of fear showed how afraid the men were; they were about to lose all hope. The storm seemed relentless, battering the sides of the boat and picking at the loosening boards still barely holding the boat together. The men began to cry out for help to God the Father, and others went to wake the Teacher who was sleeping. "Save us Lord; we are perishing." The Teacher sat up and replied, "Why are you afraid, O you of little faith?" He jumped to his feet and with confidence opened his arms to the sky. Then, shouting with a commanding voice, He rebuked the storm, the winds, and the sea. Immediately everything became calm. The men on the ship were amazed and speechless. It wasn't until somebody blurted out, "What sort of man is this, that even winds and sea obey Him?" that the tension was broken. Men began to whoop and holler in celebration. Jesus just smiled and laughed affectionately, as was His custom whenever the men engaged in jubilation, surprised by His miracles.

I AM LIKE THE DISCIPLES.

I can recall that in almost every stage of my life, there were moments of trepidation. Often, I succumb to fear. The fear was there whether it was when I was out in the dark woods when hunting as a preteen or fearful when my wife underwent open heart surgery. Sometimes I was just plain afraid to let God really move in my heart because I was fearful of what He might expose that lay deep inside of me.

Time and time again fear has proven that it can paralyze even the strongest of men. Mighty warriors have hunkered down in battle fearing for their lives. Sailors have given up all hope when a tempest overtook their ship. Falling rocks can turn the hardiest of miners into weak men afraid that the end is near. Nobody escapes life without moments of fear. But it is how we handle it that defines our true character.

I have seen a fear of death or the distress of the unknown incapacitate a person. Losing a job, a loved one, or entering a new and uncomfortable situation has brought about moments of dread. Yet I have discovered that while fear is usually debilitating, it can also be a great motivator if harnessed properly.

I attended the same elementary school from kindergarten through fourth grade. I had the same friends in each class for all of those years and I was looking forward to hanging out with most of them in fifth grade and being a student of Miss Thurston, a family friend and a fifth-grade teacher to my brother and many older friends. When it was finally my turn, I was excited about the school year. However, two weeks in I received some very bad news. Due to overpopulation of the school, and based on where I lived, I was going to have to leave my school, my friends, and my teacher and transfer to another elementary school on the other side of town.

I was devastated. At the new school I think I cried every day for at least two weeks. I'm really surprised that I didn't get labeled "cry baby," but fortunately the other kids understood what I was going through. I think they felt empathy for me because if the situation was reversed they may have felt the same way. What fueled such emotion wasn't just leaving my friends and teacher; it was a genuine fear of the unknown. It was a new place with different surroundings with nothing familiar to comfort and ease my pain.

The anxiety of moving against my will was paralyzing. I remember being embarrassed about it afterwards, but at the moment crying was the only way that I could manage my fear. As an adult, I find that change can still be scary at times, but what I didn't realize at the time was how God was going to use my apprehension for good.

I spent a full year with the fifth-grade students from Bell Anne Elementary School. I got to know them and had some great experiences. Now I had friends in both schools, and it turned out to be a blessing since we would all be going to the same junior high school. God allowed me to have new experiences, meet new friends, and He prepared me for the next step. Now instead of knowing just half of the middle-school population, I knew everybody from both groups.

I encountered a similar situation a few years ago when fear almost kept me from leaving my home church of thirty-eight years for potential ministry opportunities. God had been preparing me for ministry and I had, on numerous occasions, told Him I'd go and do whatever He asked. Yet it was hard to leave the comfort of family, friends, and my pastor, all of whom had shaped my life in so many ways. That church also prepared me for ministry. I miss them all very much, but at the same time the new experiences that God has been putting before me eases the heartache of not seeing them on a weekly basis. They will always be my friends and I'll always cherish the memories we made together, but I'm also looking forward to the new relationships and opportunities that God has planned for me and my family.

Fear, whether it is being afraid of the dark when I was a young hunter or being distressed about an upcoming change as an adult, is difficult for me. That is why I find it is important for us to encourage each other, especially during those times of consternation. Emotions can paralyze our dreams and our goals; doubts and insecurities can hold us back. I have found that fear can prohibit me from experiencing the blessings and fulfillment of plans that God has for my life. Fear comes from within, or it is sent by the evil one; either way, it is meant to keep us in bondage and to prevent us from living out a life of freedom through Jesus Christ.

Christ is a lamp for my feet and a light for my path to keep me from stumbling at night. Just as a lighthouse is a beacon for ships in the fog to guide them safely, God's hand is always there to pull me out of my darkness. His provision and protection sustain me when I am unable to stand or fight. He is with me at all times and wants me to focus only on Him, to lift my eyes to Him and to let His light shine through me and around me. Nobody needs to be afraid when standing in His light.

Life is either a daring adventure or nothing" — Helen Keller.

If you would find the men who serve God the best, you must look for the men of the most faith. Little faith will save a man, but little faith cannot do great things for God" — Charles Spurgeon.

"...for God gave us a spirit not of fear but of power and love and self-control" (*2 Timothy 1:7*).

THE STORY OF JOE BROUSSARD

Joe came from a broken home. He was an angel at home but a demon at school. His mother knew he needed a better environment so she placed him in a Christian school when he was in the fifth grade. By the eighth grade God had gotten hold of Joe, and it was then that he knew he would be called into some form of full-time ministry

Joe pursued a life of football in hopes of one day playing professional football and being used by God to share the love of Christ in that venue. But God had other plans and, instead of playing professional sports, Joe was called to minister to those professional players. God had used his life of sports to help build his ministry platform.

Joe currently serves as the National Director for Coaches Time Out (CTO), a subsidiary ministry of Pro Athletes Outreach. Before that he served in various positions with the Fellowship of Christian Athletes (FCA). He also served ten years as a pastor of college ministries at a church in Fresno, California.

Administration is one of Joe's weaknesses and he has leaned on his administrative staff while learning to respect, encourage, and elevate them throughout the years. He balances his ministry by actively using his gift of persuasion to inspire others to be involved in good things. This has helped him as a preacher, fundraiser, recruiter, and disciple.

God has used Joe's fears, doubts, and insecurities over the years to help others to know God and to follow Him fully. This is evidenced by his relationship with pro-football player and Super Bowl champion Trent Dilfer. Joe was introduced to Trent while the young player was a freshman at Fresno State. Over the last twenty years God has interwoven their lives—when Trent accepted Jesus as his Savior, when he got married, when he was drafted into the NFL, when his team won a Super Bowl, when Trent retired from professional football, and in leading his family. This relationship has been used by God to develop many other relationships with players and their spouses and has opened up ministry opportunities for Joe within professional sports.

Joe is being used by God, but he understands that it is not because of any of his own doing. He knows he will not be able to take any credit for what happens because he has relied on God and others every step of the way. He trusted God to carry him and be in every circumstance and decision. Joe has relied on mentors who encouraged him to use his gifts and to expand his ministry. He also tries to put into practice his favorite verse of Scripture, Acts 4:20: "...for we cannot but speak of what we have seen and heard." These words remind him daily why he is involved in ministry to athletes and coaches.

> *Fear is not from God. You will never truly experience your purpose until you trust God with everything, including your daily involvement in His work"*
> *—Joe Broussard, CTO National Director.*

Disciples' Areas of weakness	How God used the disciples
· Doubt · Fear · Little faith at times · Often ignorant of Jesus' plans	· To spread His saving message · To build His church · To write books of the Bible · To be witnesses of Jesus' miracles · For each one to be used in a different way

LIFE APPLICATION QUESTIONS:

(Read Matthew 4:18–22, Luke 5 and 8:22–25 for these stories about the disciples.)

1. Who were the first four disciples to be called into ministry with Jesus?
2. What illustration did Jesus use to call these men into ministry?
3. What did these men give up to follow Christ?

> *God often uses the moments in our daily lives to set up the narrative for how our life's ministry is going to unfold.*

4. In the Joe Broussard story, what main point was made?
5. When you felt that you were ready to answer God's call on your life, did you also feel waves of doubt and fear flood over you? What will help you to put that fear aside?

WHEN GOD CALLS US TO LIVE FOR HIM, IT MOST LIKELY WILL REQUIRE SOME SORT OF SACRIFICE!

Chapter Seven

LUST

The air was ripe with the first signs of spring. The days were getting longer and it was the perfect time to send out armies in defense of the kingdom and to take over cities that were becoming a dangerous threat to our people. Success had smiled brightly on us over the past year and I was becoming accustomed to everything going our way. But, I must admit, I was getting a little bored.

I sent word to Joab and his servants and pretty much all of Israel to go and lay waste the Ammonites and to seize the city of Rabbah. It was in our national interest to do so, but with all of the past battles and success we'd had, I felt I wasn't needed on the battlefield. Being king, who was going to tell me differently? So, I stayed back at the palace taking it easy. The monarchy was in good hands and it was great to be the king.

As most were off to war, the kingdom was quiet, which made the late afternoons tedious to deal with. I was tired of sitting or reclining on the couch and decided to take a walk along the rooftop. It would be a great place to get some fresh air and to look over my kingdom. Laid out before me was the most beautiful realm in this part of the world. When I think about it, we had endured a lot and it all began with defeating that giant of a man, Goliath, and waging war on the Philistines. Sure there were some minor defeats, struggles, and difficulties, but lately there were only good times.

I paced and moved around the rooftop breathing in the air and admiring all that I could see. I looked down to my right and noticed a small partition blocking a nearby patio. I leaned out over the railing a little bit and could now clearly see beyond the partition. What I saw next would change my life. The most beautiful woman I had ever laid eyes on was privately bathing on her roof. Her place was obstructed for the rest of the kingdom; only from my vantage point could she be seen. I glanced away but was drawn back by her beauty and by the lust bubbling deep inside of me. I knew I shouldn't stare, but I lingered longer than I should have. My glance now turned to a leer, and the longer I watched her the more my lust began to desire this woman. I felt conviction, but only for a second because my desires were gaining ground and my mind began to justify the actions I would eventually take.

Her privacy was an engineering mistake and her nakedness was no longer a privacy issue to my way of thinking. I had allowed my eyes, my heart, and all that I was to fall into deep lust for this woman. It was the perfect time to act, especially knowing that the other men were out doing my work in defense of the kingdom. Nobody would know and the next few days would be the perfect time to fulfill my strong desire. I sent a trusted messenger to find out more about this woman and to bring her back to me.

Later I was shocked to find out that my lustful affair with Bathsheba, the wife of Uriah the Hittite, one of my soldiers, had resulted in her becoming pregnant. My mind began to whirl, but it wasn't long before I found a way out of this mess. I was all in at this point, and Bathsheba had become an obsession, maybe even something more. To cover up the pregnancy I put my plot into motion and brought her husband home from the war. I thanked him for his war efforts and asked how the battle was going. Then I encouraged him to go and get some rest and spend the night in his house.

Instead my servants told me that Uriah had slept outside the door of my house. I summoned him into my presence and asked him why he didn't go to his own house. His response was noble and I respected the fact that he didn't want to live in luxury when his fellow soldiers were suffering difficulties in battle. My initial plan to get him to go to bed with his wife had failed, so I concocted another ruse and invited him to a party, making sure he would drink enough to forget his pledge to his fellow soldiers and to follow my plan, causing him to spend time with his wife. It couldn't be known that his wife's child wasn't his own.

He was a good soldier: he handled his drink but still he did not go down to his own house. Frustrated, I had no other choice but to make preparations for him to be sent back to his unit. I sent a sealed letter with him to give to the leader of the army, Joab. In the letter I informed Joab that he was to position Uriah near the front of battle where there was the heaviest fighting and then to have his troops draw back from Uriah, leaving him helpless and an open target for an enemy's arrow.

After some time, word made its way back to me that my plan to eliminate Uriah had succeeded. When the proper amount of time to mourn had finished, I brought Bathsheba into my house to be my wife. Then I put the matter to rest in my heart.

The object of my initial lust had now become my wife and I felt fulfilled. We were content together but God was unhappy with my actions. He sent to me a man named Nathan who told me a story that was pretty convicting. It was at that point that I broke down, but not before he pronounced God's judgment upon me. Nathan informed me that our child would die and the sword would never leave my family because I had Uriah slain. My wives would sleep with my neighbors and all of Israel would know about it.

I broke down. I had sinned against the Lord and now I was going to reap the consequences of my many sins. My confession couldn't save me from the consequences of my sins, but it would go a long way in reconciling with God. Nathan informed me that God had put my sins away and that I would not die because of my disobedience although I would suffer the consequences of the things that were about to happen to me.

Our child was born but became sick. I fasted and worshiped God in hopes that His mercy would shine upon me and my child. Seven days later the child passed away. I went to comfort Bathsheba and we mourned together. That night we conceived another son whose name would be Solomon.

I would never be able to make up for all of the pain I caused and the deceit I engaged in, but that didn't stop me from truly repenting, seeking forgiveness and becoming a man who continually seeks after God's own heart. I had suffered the consequences of my actions and, no matter how hard I tried to run from them, they would stick with me for the rest of my life; still, God's grace would always outpace them.

I AM LIKE DAVID.

I am a man who has committed adultery in my own heart and has found ways to be deceptive about the sins that lurk behind my thoughts. Fortunately, my thoughts haven't led to the murder of a man to cover up my sins, as King David did, but somewhere hidden in my heart is an evil that is just waiting to pounce.

Most men have probably gone through the same temptations as King David and me. We may ignore sin for the moment, but then we suffer the consequences and justify our actions when God convicts us. We ignore our sins for a while until we can no longer bear the pressing of the Holy Spirit. We approach God and confess our sins, experience freedom from those sins, and then spend the rest of our lives fighting off the evil one who continually tries to remind of us of our failures.

If a king, a warrior of Israel, a man of faith dedicated to serving God, and a man known for seeking after God's own heart could fall victim to lust, how much easier is it for me? David engaged in a complicated and murderous love affair; he was driven by lust to do things he probably never thought he'd do. Fortunately, God's grace overcomes confessed sin.

I have come to realize that even cheating, lying, and lust-filled manipulators can be forgiven and ultimately used by God. If God is willing to reuse them, then He is willing to reuse me too. But I also know one thing very well, if I think I can brush sexual sins like pornography, adulterous affairs, and other sins of this nature under the rug and hope God will still use me, I will be sadly mistaken. God is not looking for perfect men; He is looking for men with contrite hearts.

To be used by God requires repentance—seeking forgiveness from God and going to those who've been hurt through our inappropriate sins and asking them for forgiveness. It isn't easy, but if we want to be right with God, we will have to do it. There will be an inner struggle as we are trying to come up with the courage to confess, and there may be consequences, hurt, and pain from confessing. I have found that once I've navigated those waters, I will ask myself why I didn't do it sooner.

Scripture tells us that man's heart is naturally wicked and that all men have sinned, with the exception of Jesus. Some sins come with bigger consequences than others, but in God's eyes all are equal in nature. God doesn't choose men to serve Him based on a man's perception of the severity of his sins, but rather by the depth of a repentant heart. David had an adulterous affair and then had a man killed because of it and yet God still chose to use him. Did David suffer any consequences for his sins? Yes, but his repentance and God's forgiveness put him in a position to still be used by God.

God loves each of us and He has a plan for our lives. However, He does require us to confess our sins, seek forgiveness, and to turn away from them. Micah 6:8 says, "He has told you, O man, what is good; and what does the Lord require of you but to do justice, and to love kindness, and to walk humbly with your God?"

Once we've confessed our sins, we will likely feel the burden of sin lifted. But I have to remember that those to whom I am confessing are hearing about my sin for the first time. It takes time for them to forgive and to let go. I may be feeling burden free, but others may have been hurt and need time to heal. I may have been dealing with my sins for quite a while, but the other people haven't. I need to be understanding of their hurt. We confess our sins, get right with God, and surround our confession with gentleness and empathy.

> *The desire of love is to give. The desire of lust is to take" — Author Unknown.*

> *The righteousness of the upright delivers them, but the treacherous are taken captive by their lust" (Proverbs 11:6).*

David—Areas of weakness	How God used David
· Lust · Adultery · Killing a man to cover up his own sin	· As King of Israel · To kill Goliath · As warrior and defender of Israel · To become a man after God's own heart · As an ancestor of Jesus · As a writer of many Psalms

LIFE APPLICATION QUESTIONS:

(Read 2 Samuel 11 for more on the story of David and Bathsheba.)

1. What mistake did David make that put him in a position to be tempted by lust?
2. What action could David have immediately taken after his sin with Bathsheba that would have saved him from some long-term consequences?

> *Temptation is not a sin, but acting on the desires of that temptation is what becomes sinful. It's usually a desire hidden deep in the dark areas of the heart that eventually comes to light.*

3. Everyone will face temptation throughout their lifetime. It may be pride, anger, gluttony, or sexual desires. What is your greatest area of weakness?
4. What can you do to set up safeguards in your life to protect yourself from these temptations?
5. Do you have someone in your life with whom you can talk about your weakness, and can you count on that friend to help you through your daily struggles?

SIN IS EVERYWHERE.
TEMPTATION IS JUST AROUND THE CORNER.
ACTING OUT THOSE SINS CAN
DO DAMAGE TO OUR PRESENT
OR FUTURE RELATIONSHIPS AND MINISTRY.

Chapter Eight

DELAY

I've been in the Teacher's inner circle from the very beginning. It never gets old; it has been a unique experience. Actually, it is very humbling, and just when I think I know what He is going to do in a particular situation, He does something totally out of the box. On more than one occasion I have been left stupefied; all I could do was stare in amazement.

The other day Jesus did it again. A servant came with a dire message from a family that has been intimately involved in our ministry and had seen the miraculous acts of our Teacher. That is why they sent word to the Master that our friend was sick and dying. His sisters knew that Jesus could heal their brother, and I'm sure they were waiting anxiously for Him to arrive. But once again, He did the complete opposite of what all of us were thinking He would do. I should have realized by now that my ways are not His ways and that even though a lot of times His actions don't seem to make much sense to the rest of us, His words and His ways have always been the proper course of action.

As we began to pack our things to go, He told us to stay. Then

He said, "This illness does not lead to death. It is for the glory of God, so that the Son of God may be glorified through it." I could tell the others were as puzzled as I was, but we'd been learning to trust Him so we stayed where we were for two more days and then He said we should go to Judea. Sure, we questioned Him because we had just fled from Judea. The religious leaders there were trying to stone the Master. I could tell by the look in His eyes that our fear was misguided and He broke into another story about walking in the light.

Finally, when it came time to visit our dying friend, Lazarus, it had been days since the servant brought us word of his condition. When we arrived it was quickly apparent that Lazarus had passed away. Some of the family and friends who had shown up to grieve with the family told us that this was the fourth day since his passing. That would explain why family and friends were there, since according to Jewish custom the first three days are set aside for professional mourners to grieve. The fourth day is when things calm down quite a bit and family and close friends come to show their support.

Martha, one of Lazarus's sisters came out to meet the Teacher. They embraced in a hug and then Martha said to Jesus, "Lord, if you had been here, my brother would not have died. But even now I know that whatever you ask from God, God will give you."

He replied, "Your brother will rise again."

"I know that he will rise again in the resurrection on the last day."

"Martha, I am the resurrection and the life. Whoever believes in me, though he die, yet shall he live, and everyone who lives and believes in me shall never die. Do you believe this?"

"Yes, Lord; I believe that you are the Christ, the Son of God, who is coming into the world."

She turned and departed, mumbling something about telling her sister, Mary, that the Teacher was here. Still not totally understanding what Jesus was up to, I began to think back on His actions and what He had been saying. To begin with, He delayed when He heard that Lazarus was sick and He mentioned this illness would not end in death, but Lazarus was dead. Now the Teacher was talking to Martha about being the life and the resurrection and asking her if she believed this. I could sense that Martha was discouraged and maybe even a little disappointed that Jesus wasn't there to save her brother. But when He talked to her there was no doubt of her commitment to following Jesus.

From what we could gather, Mary had isolated herself from the others. Obviously, she was depressed and saddened over the loss of her brother, but with word that Jesus was there she perked up enough to come out and meet Him. I had never seen the Master cry before, but when He wept with them it was one of the most vulnerable emotions I had seen in Him up to this point. It was obvious that He really cared for Lazarus, Martha, and Mary. He was really moved by their grief and it showed me that Jesus loves and cares about all of us and empathizes with our hurts and needs.

What I saw next would have been unbelievable, but I saw it with my own eyes. Jesus went to Lazarus's grave and asked some men to roll away the stone. Martha spoke up and said, "Lord, by this time there will be an odor, for he has been dead four days." The Teacher quickly responded, "Did I not tell you that if you believed you would see the glory of God?" They took away the stone and Jesus began to pray out loud thanking his Father, and then he cried out in a loud voice, "Lazarus, come out."

Once again I stood there stupefied as I watched a dead man walk out of the grave bound in linen strips from head to toe. Jesus spoke again: "Unbind him, and let him go." Then the linen strips fell to the ground and there was Lazarus standing before the Master with the biggest grin I have ever seen. The Master had just brought a man back to life. Wow!

After the shock wore off, the people who had witnessed this amazing event began to talk and the chatter rose with the excitement of what had just happened. But there was a small remnant who remained silent and then quickly ran off. I went over to a man who was standing beside them and asked him what was going on. He told me that some of them were going to tell the Pharisees about what had just happened.

Much later, I would be able to piece together what this day had meant in the life of Jesus and what it would mean for us. We were learning so much from Jesus and I was looking forward to what was coming next. But, I still misunderstood why the Teacher was here on earth. I thought the Messiah was going to be our new king on earth. I was wrong, and when those men ran off to tell the Pharisees, they basically set in motion a plot to kill Jesus.

I AM LIKE MARY, MARTHA AND SOMETIMES I AM LIKE LAZARUS.

I'm like Martha because I tend to question God when He doesn't respond the way that I think He should. I'm like Mary because I isolate myself when things don't go right, often forgetting about the love of my friend, Jesus. Like them, I don't usually handle delay the way that I should.

On a recent family vacation to Yellowstone National Park we found out that delay is a common occurrence in the park. It had been a long day of sightseeing for us and it was time to get back to our lodging, get some dinner, and rest. We rounded a curve and had to hit our brakes pretty hard to avoid a log jam of vehicles that were stopped bumper to bumper. Traffic didn't move and there was no sign of oncoming traffic.

We tried to wait patiently, but with five kids and two parents tired and hungry, we didn't have time for this. After twenty minutes of sitting in the same spot we finally learned the reason for our delay. A lone bison was walking down the middle of the oncoming lane with a train of vehicles moving at a crawl behind it. There was no place to pass since our lane was filled with stopped cars, and trees lined the narrow road. Eventually we began to move and found out that a herd of bison had taken over the roadway and they were the reason for this major traffic jam. The delay turned out to be great fun because the children got to see some pretty amazing animals up close and personal.

But in general, human beings like me don't like to wait. When the car in front of me takes too long to move after the light turns green, I honk my horn. Frustration builds when traffic is slow and my anger mounts when traffic comes to a complete stop. In grocery stores I scan check-out lines looking for the shortest line possible, and at amusement parks I am willing to pay extra money to purchase a ticket for a fast-pass to the front of the line. Waiting is an inconvenience, and typically I see no merit in standing still—but God does.

In the case of Lazarus, Jesus knew the entire situation from beginning to end. He knew Lazarus's condition would not ultimately culminate in death. In John 11:4 we read the words of Jesus who said, "This illness does not lead to death. It is for the glory of God, so that the Son of God may be glorified through it." Jesus, wasn't worried because He knew that something much greater would happen as a result of His delay.

Jesus did not delay from a lack of concern; rather, it was to establish conditions for something greater. Not only would Lazarus be raised from the dead, but this moment would begin to set in motion the plot to kill Jesus and fulfill God's plan of salvation. God's ways are not our ways. The prophet Isaiah recorded God's words for us in Isaiah 55:8–9, "For my thoughts are not your thoughts, neither are your ways my ways, declares the LORD. For as the heavens are higher than the earth, so are my ways higher than your ways and my thoughts than your thoughts." Jesus delayed because He was setting the stage for His coming trial, death, and resurrection.

The delay of Jesus showed perfect timing. It was Jewish custom that the first three days be set aside for mourning. The family usually hired professional mourners and it was an intense time of grief. On day four, family and friends showed up. Mourning was less intense then and it became a more intimate time for the family to deal with their loss. So Jesus showed up exactly when He needed to be there.

The timing of Jesus is always perfect and His delays are always meant to teach us more about ourselves and more about Him. Jesus taught the disciples to walk in the light as He is in the light, and if I am grounded in Christ, I will not stumble. Jesus taught Martha that He was more than a healer and that He was God incarnate and had the power over death; He is the resurrection and the life. Jesus met Mary where she was emotionally and demonstrated that He cared for her and the family deeply. He came to her during her grief. He was troubled and deeply moved so much so that He wept. Jesus taught Mary that He is God's compassionate Son who could empathize and understand her situation.

In this story Jesus reminds me that all that He does brings glory to the Father. He thanked His Father before raising Lazarus from the dead, and in Luke 23:46, where we read about Jesus on the cross and dying a slow death, we hear him cry out, "Father, into your hands I commit my Spirit!' When He said that, He breathed his last. Christ delays to glorify His heavenly Father and in the case of Lazarus, the delay of Jesus was meant to point to something greater—His resurrection and the glory of the Father.

When delays happen in my life, I need to know that what God is doing now is preparing me for the next step. I need to acknowledge that God's ways are better than my ways and that His timing is always perfect in my life. When I trust Him during times of delay, I learn more about myself and God and, in doing so, my actions will glorify my heavenly Father. When God delays, I get ready for something greater.

> *...so Christ, having been offered once to bear the sins of many, will appear a second time, not to deal with sin but to save those who are eagerly waiting for him" (Hebrews 9:28).*

Lazarus, Mary and Martha—Areas of weakness	How God used them
· Lazarus's illness followed by death · Ignorance of God's ways—Martha · Questioning—Martha · Depressed and isolated—Mary	· To set the stage for Christ's own death, burial, and resurrection · For biblical examples to show us that God loves us · As witnesses to the miracle of raising Lazarus from the dead

LIFE APPLICATION QUESTIONS:

(Read John 11 for more of the story.)

1. What was the response of the disciples when Jesus delayed?
2. What was the response of Martha when Jesus delayed?
3. What was the response of Mary when Jesus delayed?

> *Know that when God delays in our lives it is because He knows the beginning and the end of what is happening. His ways are not our ways and His timing is always perfect.*

4. What was Jesus' response when presented with the news that Lazarus was sick?
5. What was the response of others when they witnessed the miracle that Jesus performed by raising Lazarus from the dead?
6. How do you respond to delays in your life?

WHEN GOD DELAYS IN OUR LIVES IT IS OFTEN TO TEACH US MORE ABOUT HIMSELF.

Chapter Nine

COURAGE

Behind his shield bearer, the giant Philistine moved forward, shouting to the handsome youth who stood his ground. "Am I a dog that you come to me with sticks?" he said. This man, who stood head and shoulders above the tallest man in the Israelite army, continued cursing this young man who dared challenge him in battle.

Goliath was the champion of the Philistine army, and no ordinary man would dare challenge this warrior in a fight. In fact, the Israelites, who were camped on the side of a mountain with a valley separating them and the Philistine garrison, had been stalled for forty days before a lowly shepherd boy took up Goliath's winner-take-all challenge.

David, the youngest of all of the sons of Jesse, wore no armor. He carried only a staff, a sling, and five smooth stones in his shepherd's pouch. Goliath, on the other hand, wore a bronze helmet and a bronze coat of mail to protect his midsection. His legs were also covered in bronze armor and he carried a large heavy javelin with an iron tip.

The only reason David even showed up at the front lines of battle was to obey his father who had sent him on a mission to take some things to his three brothers who were fighting for King Saul's army. On the day David arrived, the giant, Goliath, was again announcing his daily challenge aimed at the Israelites, which he had been doing arrogantly for the past thirty-nine days. He demanded that their best fighter come out and face him. The victor would rule over the losing army. Goliath taunted the Israelites with braggadocio: "I defy the ranks of Israel this day. Give me a man that we may fight together." He continued, "Why have you not come out to draw up for battle? Am I not a Philistine, and are you not servants of Saul? Choose a man for yourselves, and let him come down to me. If he is able to fight with me and kill me, then we will be your servants. But, if I prevail against him and kill him, then you shall be our servants and serve us."

David was angry that Goliath had been doing this for so long and no one had the courage to face him. He was dismayed that the Israelite army had cowered in fear for over a month, afraid of this giant. David, the shepherd boy, began asking questions about Goliath's challenge and his words were brought to King Saul who then called for David to stand before him. David responded to Saul with these words, "Let no man's heart fail because of him. Your servant will go and fight with this Philistine."

King Saul questioned his ability and youth, but David stood his ground and responded by telling the king of the lions and bears he had killed while tending sheep. He reiterated, "The LORD who delivered me from the paw of the lion and from the paw of the bear will deliver me from the hand of this Philistine." Saul responded, "Go, and the LORD be with you!"

Goliath shouted as he moved forward, "Come to me, and I will give your flesh to the birds of the air and to the beasts of the field."

David was unfazed by the babblings of this giant man and shouted back, "You come to me with a sword and with a spear and with a javelin, but I come to you in the name of the LORD of Hosts, the God of the armies of Israel, whom you have defied. This day the LORD will deliver you into my hand, and I will strike you down and cut off your head. And I will give the dead bodies of the host of the Philistines this day to the birds of the air and the wild beasts of the earth, that all the earth may know that there is a God in Israel, and that all this assembly may know that the LORD saves not with sword and spear. For the battle is the LORD's, and he will give you into our hand."

David sprang toward the mighty giant, reached his hand into his pouch and pulled out one smooth stone. The rock flew from the simple weapon and struck his enemy in the forehead. The warrior didn't even know what hit him. He fell face down on the ground. David ran over to the giant, pulled out his sword, and his words to the giant soon came true.

I WANT TO BE LIKE YOUNG DAVID

I want to be like a young David, a man willing to stand up and do something nobody else has the courage to do. I want to be a man who understands who his God really is and the power He truly possesses. I want to be a person who still has the faith of a child, but the courage of an adult warrior, a man willing to overcome personal ridicule, resigned to the fact that there isn't any doubt that God will be with him. A lowly shepherd took down a mighty giant, not because he was stronger but because he had courage, and a passion for serving the Lord. David knew what had to be done, and he didn't let the fears of his brothers, other soldiers, or even the king distract him from what he knew had to be done. Most importantly, he walked into battle with the knowledge that the Lord of hosts was with him every step of the way.

David understood that obstacles affecting God's people or interfering with God's plans needed to removed, and he was willing to do so even if it meant his own death. He wasn't going to stand idly by and allow his countrymen to be paralyzed by this single man, even if he was a giant. I'm sure he thought something like, "The bigger they are, the harder they fall."

There are times in life when obstacles press down on us and we feel immobilized under the weight of them, but these are the times when we need to find the courage to battle until victory has been won. As Winston Churchill once said, "This is the lesson: never give in, never give in, never, never, never, never—nothing, great or small, large or petty— never give in except to convictions of honor and good sense. Never yield to force; never yield to the apparently overwhelming might of the enemy."

Courage is not just for battle, but for everyday life too. Courage is used when a young boy must shinny up a steel girder to the top of an old bridge in order to enjoy the thirty-foot freefall into the refreshing river below because of the many others who had gone before him. Or the young girl who transferes schools and has no friends going into the first day of school.

What about the old man who is now a widower and must learn to cope without his wife of 60 years? Courage gets us through the trying times and even the times when we don't want to miss out on the fun. Courage is taking a job that doesn't make sense to anyone else. It often comes with risk, but when all of the factors have been considered, courage means doing the right thing.

Courage is found in unlikely places
—J.R.R. Tolkien.

Have I not commanded you? Be strong and courageous. Do not be frightened, and do not be dismayed, for the LORD your God is with you wherever you go" (Joshua 1:9).

Young David—Areas of weakness	How God used a young David
· He wasn't yet big enough to wear the king's armor · He was just a shepherd boy · He had no experience in battle	· To inspire others to do the right thing · To defeat a giant who had paralyzed the Israelite army · To prepare him to one day be king · To display courage at its highest level

LIFE APPLICATION QUESTIONS:

(Read I Samuel 17 to learn more about the battle between the young, courageous David and Goliath.)

1. What drove a young David to face the giant warrior by himself?
2. What skills or experience did a young David have in fighting the enemy?
3. Why was a young David no match for Goliath?

> *Courage is found in the depths of one's soul. You must reach for it. Not everyone uses it, but everyone has it.*

4. How did David's victory prepare him for his future role as king?
5. What is the biggest obstacle or personal enemy that you need to defeat?
6. What is standing in the way of your mustering enough courage to defeat this enemy?

LIFE IS FILLED WITH MANY GIANTS TO OVERCOME. YOU MAY JUST BE AVERAGE, BUT GOD CAN MAKE YOU INTO SOMETHING BIGGER AND STRONGER.

Chapter Ten

VALOR

The rocks were difficult to climb, so the steep cliff delayed the inevitable. Sweat covered my face and adrenaline pumped in my body. This would not be the first, but it would definitely be the biggest battle of my life. For most people this would look like a suicide run; for me it was something else, a calling much bigger than myself and a once-in-a-lifetime defining moment.

The enemy garrison, situated strategically on top of a rocky crag known as Bozez, would not be easily overcome. Armed with plowshares, mattocks, axes, and sickles, our farmers, just recently turned soldiers, would be outmatched against our enemy's more sophisticated weapons of swords, spears, and shields. Only two of us in our army had these kinds of weapons: my father, the king, and me.

My father thought it best for us to position ourselves in and around the Pomegranate cave. I found myself questioning his passive decisions of late. I'm not sure if it was because he was chastised by the prophet Samuel for being impatient and performing the peace offering and burnt sacrifice without him, or if it was something else that was holding the king's courage at bay.

I heard Samuel scold him: "You have done foolishly. You have not kept the command of the LORD your God, with which he commanded you. For then the LORD would have established your kingdom over Israel forever. But now your kingdom shall not continue. The LORD has sought out a man after his own heart, and the LORD has commanded him to be prince over his people, because you have not kept what the LORD commanded you."

Since then my father, Saul, and his army of about six hundred, had hunkered down in their cavernous holes, just waiting.

I couldn't take it anymore and I did something bold without anyone knowing about it. I went over to my armor-bearer and said, "Come, let us go over to the garrison of these uncircumcised. It may be that the LORD will work for us, for nothing can hinder the LORD from saving by many or by few."

My armor-bearer replied, "Do all that is in your heart. Do as you wish. Behold, I am with you heart and soul." His response was filled with confidence and it encouraged my soul. He had spent many a battle with me and his loyalty and trust were greatly appreciated. He often told me that I was a good man and a great warrior. He said that even the Philistines knew of my heroics in battle.

My strategy was to put ourselves in a position to be seen by the enemy and to wait for their response. If they told us to wait until they came to us, we would hold our ground; but if they dared us to come up to them and fight, then we would consider that to be the sign that God was with us. We told no one of our plan; nobody was even aware that we had gone missing.

Now we were nearing the top of the cliff. Even after the arduous climb, I felt stronger than ever. My armor-bearer was right behind me as we crested the ridge with our weapons drawn and ready for battle. When we had shown ourselves to our enemies down below, the Philistines taunted us by saying in mocking voices, "Look, those

Hebrews are coming out of their holes where they have hidden themselves." Now we stood face to face with the men we would kill in our first strike.

Our enemy approached confidently and I easily laid into the first attacker. He fell by my sword and my armor-bearer finished him off. The second attacker tried a different approach, but to no avail. Once again my loyal servant extinguished any final breath the combatant might take. Together we worked flawlessly and easily laid waste to the first strike from the enemy horde. We left a bloody trail of dead bodies, twenty men to be exact, before God made His presence known in support of our courage.

The Lord unleashed panic in our enemy, and a frightening earthquake that even made us tremble in fear. The Philistine army started attacking itself, making our task that much easier. I looked down toward the Israelite army and could see that they were beginning to figure out what was happening. It wouldn't be long before they reached our location and joined in the battle. Death was about to be unleashed again. God was on our side; victory would soon be ours.

I WANT TO BE LIKE JONATHAN.

Jonathan is a great example of a righteous man being as bold as a lion. He was a great warrior for the Israelites, and he was also trusting, courageous, and discerning. What is most inspiring about Jonathan is not only his love and loyalty to his friends, especially David, but his undeniable trust that God would have his back. Jonathan was a man of faith.

His mission wasn't a suicide pact with his armor-bearer, or even a righteous vendetta; rather, it was a battle of conviction. He went into this decision with wisdom, discernment, and by making sure that God was a part of it before he blindly took on an enemy garrison by himself. He wasn't stupid. Jonathon knew that God had to be in it.

The trust of his armor-bearer is a great testimony to the type of man Jonathan was. People typically don't follow lunatics into battle. Jonathan's faith, core beliefs, convictions, and actions spoke volumes about the type of man he was. For that, his armor-bearer had complete trust in his master's decisions. Jonathan knew his mission, overcame the obstacles standing in his way, and inspired others to come alongside him.

A few years ago we were on a family vacation when our five-year-old son taught me a spiritual lesson that I have used numerous times in my speaking and writing ministries.

It was a beautiful summer day and we had spent most of the day by the lake. But the seven of us were looking for more adventure so we took a walk. We followed a trail that led us to the back side of the lake where gigantic boulders had been strewn down the side of a mountain, spilling into the lake. About twenty people were gathered on these rocks and a few were taking the plunge into the cold, dark water below, but not all of them. Our children were eager to join in the fun, but it wasn't going to be suitable for the three youngest. So I checked it out and decided that our two oldest could participate but it was too dangerous for the others. The water was deep and we didn't have a life jacket for our five-year-old. There were large boulders to climb over just to get to the jumping spot. This was no place for a five-year-old boy, or was it?

After about twenty minutes of wearing his mother and me down, we finally relented thinking Seth would chicken out, but he was a determined little fellow. I helped him climb over the obstacles and brought him to the edge. I could see in his face that he was going to jump. The crowd began to murmur, probably wondering if he was going to jump. I had no choice but to jump in first and snag him as soon as he hit the water.

Treading water below, I watched as Seth sprang off the ledge and plummeted into the water, covering me with a tidal wave. As soon as I could see again, I reached for him as he paddled much like a dog would. He was grinning from ear to ear.

There will be times in our lives when people will tell us that we can't do something. They will be negative, or they will project their own lack of faith and their failure onto our situation. Either way they will tell us why something can't be done. Most of the criticism may come from those closest to us. Jesus said, as we read in Mark 6:4, "A prophet is not without honor, except in his hometown and among his relatives and in his own household." When we step out in faith to serve God, we have to be ready for criticism, especially if God is calling us to something that doesn't make sense to anyone else except ourselves and God.

Even grown men can aspire to be like my five-year-old son, Seth, and know what it is that they are called to do and just go for it. Jay Dennis and Jim Henry, in their book *Dangerous Intersections*, wrote, "Your passion about God's calling on your life must exceed the negativity of those who feel called to tell you why it can't be done, and it must be greater than Satan's daily darts thrown at you to discourage and distract."

Seth not only had to face his father and mother telling him that he couldn't do it, but he also had to overcome the difficult obstacles that stood in his way. When he did, he was able to reap the benefits and the enjoyment of engaging in his great adventure. The best part of his feat was that he inspired others in the crowd to say, "If that little boy can do it, so can I." Seth moved other people to action by going first and being a great example of perseverance.

Like Jonathan, David, and Seth, I want to be a man who knows my mission, can put aside the negativity of others, overcome any obstacles, make sure God is in it, and engage in my calling. Along the way maybe I'll inspire others to do the same.

> *Your passion about God's calling on your life must exceed the negativity of those who feel called to tell you why it can't be done, and it must be greater than Satan's daily darts thrown at you to discourage and distract —Jay Dennis and Jim Henry,* Dangerous Intersections.

> *The wicked flee when no one pursues, but the righteous are bold as a lion* (Proverbs 28:1).

Jonathan and David areas of weakness	How God used Jonathan and David
· They were outnumbered	· As military leaders · To kill the enemies of Israel, the Philistines · To display valor, and a trust in God that is unparalleled · To be perfect examples of how we are to live for God—fully trusting Him

LIFE APPLICATION QUESTIONS:

(Read 1 Samuel 14 for more on the story of Jonathan and his armor-bearer.)

1. Describe in your own words what fueled the passion inside of Jonathan to act with such valor.
2. Why were the Philistines at such a disadvantage in this fight with Jonathan and his armor-bearer?
3. Was it uncommon for Jonathan to act with valor? Can you list other instances?

> *Faith can move mountains and defeat our biggest enemy, but it requires a real trust in God. If we truly believe God to be who we say He is, then why do we even question that God has our back?*

4. What attributes do you like about Jonathan that are presented in this story?
5. What did Jonathan do before climbing the rocks to defeat the Philistines?
6. Do you connect with God through prayer and Bible study before you make a bold leap for Him?

SOMETIMES GOD WANTS US TO JUST GO FOR IT, BUT ONLY WHEN WE CHECK IN WITH HIM FIRST AND MAKE SURE HE IS IN WHATEVER WE ARE ABOUT TO DO.

Chapter Eleven

RUNAWAY

It was late morning and the salt from the sweat on my brow began to sting my eyes. My lungs were heavy from the many miles that I had already run, but I wasn't about to stop until I reached the port city. Many of the ships would be setting sail to get a good start on their long journeys, so if I hurried, I might find a ship willing to transport me to a place far from here.

The smell was typical of a seafaring port, part fish and alcohol, and the rest body odor from the men who had been working long days at sea. I approached every boat in the harbor hoping someone would allow me to board for a nominal fee. My destination was Tarshish, far away from this place. Now I was out of options, except for one last boat. I approached the gangplank as an old crusty-looking seafarer came walking down it. I pleaded my case to him and hoped that he would take pity on me and let me come aboard. To my surprise, he said, "Welcome to the Sea Ripper!" I paid the man, thanked him and climbed on board. I settled down below for the long trip ahead. Exhausted from the long run, I quickly fell asleep.

Sometime later, I was awakened by an angry voice. "What do

you mean, you sleeper? Get up! Call out to your god! Perhaps your god will give a thought to us so that we will not perish." I stood to my feet and could now feel the boat rocking back and forth; then I was slammed against the wall. Screams were coming from above as the crew battled a raging storm. This wasn't any ordinary storm, as evidenced by the crew's fear. In hopes of saving the ship and their lives the men were throwing supplies, gear, and anything else that wasn't attached to the ship, overboard.

From the power of this sea tempest I knew that this storm was aimed at me by my heavenly Creator. The men on the ship were superstitious men and cast lots to see who was responsible for this evil. Before it even happened, I knew the lot would fall on me. I was the one who had told God no and then tried to flee from His presence. What was I thinking?

I told the men to throw me overboard, but they weren't quite ready to do that. They attempted to row back to land and the men pulled on their oars with all of their might, but to no avail. When they gave up, I said to them once more, "Pick me up and hurl me into the sea; then the sea will quiet down for you, for I know it is because of me that this great tempest has come upon us." Afraid to look me in the eye, the men grabbed me and threw me over the railing into the raging sea below.

As soon as I hit the water, the sea instantly transformed from a raging wave to a peaceful and quiet calm. When I surfaced I could hear the men on the ship praising my God and calling out to Him. That put a smile on my face until I felt the massive body of an enormous water creature swim just below my dangling feet. I began to swim toward shore, not that I would ever make it—but I had to do something to escape the behemoth lurking in the waters below.

In a state of panic, I swam as fast as my arms and legs could muster, but I was losing ground. Then I realized that I was swimming in a wave that was moving backward. How could that be? I looked over my shoulder and could see a giant mouth opening up around me. It was going to swallow me. I kicked one last time and then I began to slip deeper into the mouth and now the throat of this giant fish. As I slid down the inner linings of the monster's throat, I threw up as the smell hit my nostrils. It felt like my nose was on fire. I fell for what seemed like an eternity and then came to a soft landing with my face slamming into a soft, sticky, and smelly substance. It was dark, but not pitch black as the creature's stomach walls had a little transparency to them letting in just a faint amount of light. I could feel the great fish begin to dive deeper into the sea. As he did, the luminescence of the walls became darker. In a few seconds the depth of the sea blocked out any remaining light and now it was pitch black.

I slowly adjusted to the smell and it no longer seemed so strong. That was a relief in and of itself. I wondered how long it might take for the fish's stomach to slowly digest me. Would it be painful? The first few hours were filled with panic and questions concerning my own death in the stomach of a giant fish. After that I settled down, realizing that my speculation was doing no good anyway. I made myself comfortable and leaned up against the side of the stomach lining. I closed my eyes, only to be hit by the sound of rushing water as a small wave struck me in the face, covering me with kelp.

At the end of the third night in the belly of that fish I was still alive. I called out to God having recognized my sin and disobedience in saying no to God and trying to flee from His calling on my life. When I had exhausted my words from seeking forgiveness, I suddenly found myself blinded by the morning light as I flew through the air and landed with a splash where the water and the beach met. God heard my prayer, saving me from a watery hell and prison, sparing my life.

I jumped back into the sea for a moment to wash my clothes from all of the fish slime. As I emerged from the water the word of the Lord came to me saying, "Arise, go to Nineveh, that great city, and call out against it the message that I tell you." So I started walking towards Nineveh, thankful that God had saved me and ready to do what God had called me to do. I would preach repentance. Yet, due to my stubborn heart, it wouldn't be the last lesson that I would have to learn.

I AM LIKE JONAH.

I'm a man who sometimes runs and tries to hide when God asks me to do the uncomfortable. I don't always have the best attitude and sometimes I make judgments when it is really God's place to decide. I guess I'm a runner!

Like Jonah, I've tried to run and hide from God's presence. I've found that there are usually two reasons why people run from God. The first is that they are convicted of sin and find that being in the presence of a holy God is extremely uncomfortable. The second is fear of the unknown. What will God ask me to do? What will it require and what kind of sacrifices will I have to make? I am afraid of being used by God because I tend to put the calling and the pressure of succeeding squarely on my own shoulders instead of letting God do His work through me.

There was a time in my life when, like Jonah, I too resisted the convicting power of God. I tried to ignore it, but He kept on pressing. I tried to occupy myself with other thoughts, and whenever I would be reminded of my disobedience, would find some justification to ignore having to deal with it. One time I battled with God for well over two years until I finally gave in. I had already asked God to forgive me soon after the sin, but my running away occurred when God pressed me to confess and seek forgiveness from others.

The terror of having to tell others wreaked havoc on my soul. I didn't want to do it. I even told God no. Even though I tried to conceal it, God's love for me was persistent and, in the end, just like Jonah, I relented. I confessed my sin to those who needed to know and after it was all over I wished I had done it sooner. It would have saved me years of anguish. Forgiveness by God and others is freeing, and God has brought extreme good out of the situation. Oh, how different it might have been had I not tried to run.

In Psalm 139:1–7, King David wrote so poetically:

> *O LORD, you have searched me and known me! You know when I sit down and when I rise up; you discern my thoughts from afar. You search out my path and my lying down and are acquainted with all my ways. Even before a word is on my tongue, behold, O LORD, you know it altogether. You hem me in, behind and before, and lay your hand upon me. Such knowledge is too wonderful for me; it is high; I cannot attain it. Where shall I go from your Spirit? Or where shall I flee from your presence?*

It is hard to run from the God who created me, knows me intimately, and knows what is in my heart before it even comes out.

Jonah is the perfect example of a reluctant misfit. He had a righteous attitude toward those to whom God called him to speak and to try to get them to repent. Jonah ran from God, and even after he finally gave in, we read later in the book of Jonah about his having another bad attitude that God had to deal with. I'd like to condemn Jonah for that, but then I would be a hypocrite because I've done the same thing. When I read about the Israelites losing faith, or griping to God about their circumstances after He had just parted the Red Sea for them, it tends to frustrate me. Then I remember that I do the same thing. My mother-in-law has a great saying when this topic comes up: "Well, it looks like another lap in the desert for us."

God's love for us is relentless, and if He is seeking us then there is no running that can ever distance us from His pursuit. When God chases after me there is no hiding place that will ever keep me from His presence. And, when God finds me, there is nothing that could ever separate me from His love.

> *God wants the whole person and He will not rest until He gets us in entirety. No part of the man will do — A.W. Tozer.*

> *Blessed are those whose way is blameless, who walk in the law of the LORD! Blessed are those who keep His testimonies, who seek him with their whole heart (Psalm 119:1–2).*

THE STORY OF TREVOR RUBLE

Trevor, a man leading a national fishing ministry called "Hooked for Life," is an educator who at one time was uncertain about the direction his life was going. He was looking for purpose and God's will, all the while struggling with self-confidence and looking for a fatherly role model who wouldn't disappoint him. When God became that person in Trevor's life, He used Trevor's passion for teaching and fishing to reveal His Son, Jesus Christ, to others through a national fishing ministry.

A key verse that Trevor relies on is 1 Peter 4:10, which says, "As each has received a gift, use it to serve one another, as good stewards of God's varied grace." Trevor has taken hold of this verse and allowed God to use him to become a fisher of men.

> *Our passion for adventure gives us a tool or platform through which we can best reach others for Christ —Trevor Ruble.*

Jonah areas of weakness	How God used Jonah
· He was stubborn · He was angry · He tried to run from God · He was ignorant of God's mercy · He felt he knew what was best not what God thought was best	· To spare Nineveh from God's wrath and punishment · As a biblical example of what not to do

LIFE APPLICATION QUESTIONS:

(Read the book of Jonah for more of this story.)

1. Why do you think Jonah refused to do what God asked?
2. Have you ever felt God calling you to do something but you refused?

> *Fortunately, God is patient with us when we refuse to do what He asks. Still we run the risk of getting passed over and missing out on the blessing He has for us if we don't ultimately step out and do what He is calling us to do.*

3. If you have said no to God, what has been the result?
4. Have you ever asked God to forgive you for saying no?
5. What could you do to rectify the situation or to re-engage in your ministry calling?

YOU CAN RUN BUT YOU CAN'T HIDE FROM GOD! TURN BACK TO GOD AND MAKE IT EASY ON YOURSELF.

Chapter Twelve

STRONG

The young lion roared, then sprang from his hiding place in the vineyards, charging directly at me. I steadied my feet and braced for the collision. As the attacker leapt through the air, I felt a supernatural surge flow through my body; in that moment I knew that I could take on this beast.

With my right fist I punched as hard as I could, crushing the throat of my attacker. His loud roar became a gargled concoction of wheezing and gasping for breath. The lion was stunned, but still tried to take me down. His claws cut into my back; immediately I followed with my left arm, swinging around his neck and putting him in a choke hold. Without even thinking, I plunged my right fist deep into his throat, tearing and pulling out flesh. I had the lion's esophagus in my hands and ripped it out. I didn't stop there. I ripped this beast from limb to limb until he was unrecognizable, leaving his remains on the side of the road for the vultures to enjoy.

I continued down the road while the supernatural adrenaline rush began to subside. It was an amazing feeling, one I hope to experience again. My parents had told me that I was special and that I was on a mission to do the work of God, but I hadn't been told what that plan was. Until it became clearer, I was going to meet this woman who had caught my eye and to ask her father for her hand in marriage.

The meeting with her and her father went well. After a few days I went back home to tell my parents and begin the preparations for the wedding. As, I passed through the area where I had been attacked by the lion, I came across its carcass. There was a swarm of bees inside the body, filling it with honey. I received a few bee stings as I scraped out the honey, but the pain was well worth the reward. I took the honey back to my parents but I didn't tell them what I had done with the lion or where the honey came from.

When it was time for the wedding, I traveled with my father and mother down to the young woman's family for the customary seven-day feast. While celebrating, I proposed a challenge to thirty companions at the feast. It was a riddle, and if they could figure it out in the seven days before the feast ended then I would provide them with thirty linen garments and thirty changes of clothes. If they could not figure it out, then I would receive thirty linen garments and changes of clothes from them. They agreed to the challenge and worked to solve the following riddle:

Out of the eater came something to eat.
Out of the strong came something sweet.

Over the next few days my wife pressed me hard to tell her the answer to the riddle, since her people had threatened to burn her father's house because they were about to become impoverished after I beat them in this challenge. She was relentless, so on the seventh day I caved in and told her the riddle's solution. She then went out and told her people and they came and answered my riddle correctly:

What is sweeter than honey?
What is stronger than a lion?

Realizing how they had used my wife and even threatened her, the supernatural rush came over me once more. I went down to another town and struck down thirty Philistines, taking their garments, and returned to give them to those thirty companions. When I returned, my father-in-law had given my wife away to my best man because he thought I hated my wife. He then offered me his youngest daughter.

It was becoming clearer to me why God had infused me with such strength and power. It was to judge the Philistines for ruling over the Israelites for forty years and to punish them for their evil deeds. I went out and began trapping foxes. I caught three hundred of them, tying together the tails of each pair and fastening a torch between their tails. I lit each torch on fire and sent the foxes out into the fields of the Philistines that were ready for harvest. One hundred and fifty pairs of foxes were let loose across the countryside; the smoke and flames from the burning fields could be seen for miles.

It was an inferno of epic proportions, and my mission to punish the Philistines that began as a small flame was now roaring into a blazing-hot fire. It was consuming everything in its path, and this was just the beginning. I haven't always been perfect and I wouldn't always make the right choices along the way, but God has chosen to use me anyway. In my case, it was to serve as judge and jury.

I AM LIKE SAMSON

I don't have Samson's muscles but I'm a man willing to surrender his spiritual gifts to God who loves this world. A man easily seduced by the beauty of sin, I'm also a man who often doesn't realize how he is equipped with God's strength. A man like me might be empowered to move the world, yet hesitate to assume that power.

In the summer of 2013, I had the privilege of picking up Walt Wiley, former team chaplain of the Atlanta Braves, from Detroit's Metro airport. My wife and I serve on the steering committee for the Coaches Time Out conference (CTO), a conference designed to encourage coaches and their spouses. The conference is sponsored by Professional Athletes Outreach (PAO) and Score Ministries. Walt was to be one of the main speakers at the Great Lakes event, and I had volunteered to pick him up when his flight arrived. I am so glad that I did.

During our long ride to the hotel, I had a great conversation with Walt and his wife, Patti. They were extremely encouraging, although I had to laugh the following day at the conference when Walt asked me who I was. I laughed and said, "How could you forget that Mike Tison drove you to your hotel?" Then he laughed and it became a running joke all weekend. Walt was a great speaker and had so many good points during his time on the platform, but the point I remember the most happened in the car ride on the way to the hotel.

Patti and Walt asked me what I did for a living. When they found out I was in ministry, that opened up all kinds of questions and discussions. Something came up about trying to maximize my strengths and balance my weaknesses as I attempted to serve the Lord. I'll never forget what Walt said: "Your biggest weakness in life is your greatest strength pushed to an extreme."

One of my strengths is that I am willing to do things for people when they ask. I like to help others but I have trouble saying, "No." Then my schedule and these kinds of opportunities overwhelm me, and what is my greatest strength is pushed to its limit. Then ministry suffers or I get distracted because I have too many things going on. What is a gift of encouraging and helping people can become overwhelming, limiting and ultimately hindering my effectiveness when it is pushed to the extreme.

I've found that it is important to understand both my strengths and my weaknesses if I want to be effective for God. Samson was a man of great strength, but even he had moments of failure and these were areas in his life where he was spiritually weak. If God was willing to use a man like Samson, then surely He is willing to use a man like me.

INFERNO

The day was cloudy and overcast, and it set the mood for boredom. Coming after an already gloomy winter, we were three young boys eager to go outside and play. Spring fever had infected us and we were itching to do something.

Our plan was set into motion. We gathered at the rally point, in a clump of trees across a field and many acres from the nearest house. It was a place free of any disturbance. The only inconvenience was from the gusting wind, making communication between the three of us extremely difficult.

One of my friends pulled a lighter out of his pocket and lit little patches of weeds, creating mini-fires before quickly stomping them out. He passed the lighter to another boy who eagerly followed suit. The dead weeds, lacking moisture due to a dry spring, were the perfect kindling for boys playing with fire.

The forty- to-fifty-mile-an-hour wind gusts started swirling, making for big flames. We were having a great time. Then the wind fanned one particular small flame into a medium-sized fire that started to make us nervous. All three began to stomp on the growing fire. The flame couldn't be stopped and continued to spread, growing larger and larger. Weeds disintegrated in the rising flames. Frantic, we three boys tried everything to extinguish the blaze, even throwing dirt on it in hopes of putting it out.

One of us stayed to put out the fire; the other two ran to get help. Sprinting down the trail we formulated a plan to tell our parents in hopes of getting ourselves out of the mess we had created. The accidental fire was gaining strength and we could hear the crackling of flames behind us. Looking back we could see our lone firefighting friend running frantically to catch up to us as a wall of flame climbed higher into the sky. Flames licked at his heels as he fled the out-of-control inferno.

The local fire department was called to put out what began as a small flame only to grow into a wildfire.

A LESSON LEARNED

Three boys learned a lesson that day. God places in us spiritual gifts. Those gifts lie at the bottom of our souls like small embers waiting for oxygen to be fanned into flame. God is intentional when He knits a person together for His purposes. His sovereignty places us in this universe with perfect timing and precise location. He controls the flame that He ignites in us through the gifts He gives us, fanning our spiritual fire.

I often ask men, "How has God wired you? Do you know? Have you ever thought about it?" It's important to identify what God has placed inside of us so that we can better understand how He wants to fulfill the plans that He has for our lives. We all have some gift, and the best way to begin using that gift is through prayer. We need to ask God to help us discover our gifts and talents and to uncover our personality traits. It is important that we and God are both on the same page. A committed prayer time will help reveal what makes us tick and what we have been designed to do.

> *For you formed my inward parts; you knitted me together in my mother's womb. I praise you, for I am fearfully and wonderfully made. Wonderful are your works; my soul knows it very well (Psalm 139:13–14).*

Spend time in communication with God. He knows exactly how you are wired. Remember that God knew you before you were even shaped in your mother's womb. He knows everything about you from beginning to end and He knows all the details of your life.

> *The LORD will keep you from all evil; he will keep your life. The LORD will keep your going out and your coming in from this time forth and forevermore (Psalm 121:7–8).*

SELF-EXAMINATION

The next step comes with self-examination. It is important for every man who follows Jesus to understand himself and to tap into the gifts God has given him. Everybody has them; maybe you just haven't found yours yet. But you will never find them if you don't go looking for them. Self-examination is central in this process. After God, who really knows you the best? You do.

Most men are well aware of what is inside them; sometimes it is just a matter of taking the time to sit down and write them out. That will allow you to be able to prioritize them and then put a plan into place that will complement the adventure God has designed for you. But this part of the process of finding your gifts begins with an open, honest, and introspective reflection about how God has wired you. You know what secrets you're hiding and what needs to be confessed. You know what excites you and what deflates you, so why not take advantage of what you know about yourself and examine who you are in a fair and objective way.

Then take what you learn about yourself back to God in prayer. Confess if you need to, but ask God to help you work through your deficiencies and to open doors so that you can start implementing ministry that aligns with your personality traits, skills, and talents.

Take the torch and light the sky,
Lift up your eyes and see, the fields look white
to me.
Get up! Get Up!
The Time. The time is right now.
Wake up, Shake up, the world and be a light now.
Come on! Shine on!
It's time to do something about it all.
How about it starts right now.
—From the song Get Up, Get Up *by Christian*
recording artist Luke Cyrus

For this reason I remind you to fan into flame the gift of God, which is in you through the laying on of my hands, for God gave us a spirit not of fear but of power and love and self-control
(2 *Timothy* 1:6–7).

Samson—Areas of weakness	How God used Samson
· He was a ladies' man —Lust · He did not always follow the Lord's ways · Sometimes revenge ruled his heart	· As a deliverer and protector of Israel · As one of the judges of the Old Testament · He had a strong faith in God

LIFE APPLICATION QUESTIONS:

(Read 2 Timothy 1 and 2 for more insight on using your gifts for God.)

1. Do you know what your spiritual strengths are? If so, write them out below.
2. Describe your personality traits using only a single word for each trait.

> *God has gifted you and it is your responsibility to learn how He has wired you for service. Begin to explore your gifts and God will reveal His plan for your life.*

3. List your personal strengths and weaknesses as you see them.
4. List any fears or obstacles you believe may be holding you back from seizing the adventure God has for you.
5. List the major reasons why you feel unqualified to serve God.
6. Take a black marker and in large letters write over the answers in question numbers four and five with three large and bold words—"God Qualifies Me!"

WHEN IN DOUBT ABOUT YOUR CALLING, KNOW THAT GOD ALWAYS POSITIONS YOU FOR SUCCESS AND NOT FOR FAILURE!

Chapter Thirteen

MISSION

There might be some who would say, "I was reluctant", but it would be false. If you called me a misfit, that would be a better description, but you should never say I was reluctant. After all it's not too often that a man lives in the wilderness clothed in camel's hair with his one luxury item being a leather belt pulled tightly around his waist, and his favorite foods being crunchy locusts and wild honey. I'm a hunter and gatherer, and there is no better place for me than to be out in God's creation alone except when I'm getting stung.

I am not a demon as some would say; I like to refer to myself as an outdoorsman, a man of the wild, a little crazy but an introvert on a mission. The prophet of old Isaiah said,"I am the voice of one crying out in the wilderness." I guess that would make me a herald, a public speaker, or an evangelist telling others to make straight the way of the Lord. I have followers, my own disciples, but we all know that I am nothing more than a single drop of water preparing the way for a massive flood of righteousness that will wash over this fallen world.

It is a calling that I take very seriously and as a result have sacrificed much in order to spend time with God being equipped for the ministry at hand, which is to announce the coming Messiah. I'm a mountain man, baptizing others coming into faith and gladly sharing the exciting news even if I have to do it while sleeping on the ground or eating bugs.

When I'm not living in the wild, I spend most of my time baptizing new believers along the Jordan River near the town of Bethany or just -out preaching in the wilderness of Judea. It was here when the religious leaders of the day, the Pharisees and the Sadducees, came to me for baptism. I baptized them, but not without warning. I called them a brood of vipers and asked them who had warned them to flee the coming wrath to come? I told them they should bear fruit after their repentance and not look to their historical Jewish ancestry as a means of salvation. I then explained in a short parable that even now an axe is laid to the root of the trees. If the tree does not bear good fruit it is cut down and thrown into the fire.

I told them that I baptize for repentance but there is one coming after me who is greater than I. He is someone whose sandals I'm not even worthy to carry, someone who will baptize with the Holy Spirit and with fire. The threshing floor will be cleared and the wheat gathered into the barn, but he will burn the chaff that remains with unquenchable fire. I baptized them all, but I'm not really sure if they truly understood or even took to heart the meaning of what they were doing. Obviously, it is not my call. I'll leave that up to God.

Time passed, and again I was baptizing along the Jordan River when the Great Light appeared to me and asked me to baptize Him. "I need to be baptized by you, and do you come to me?" I implored of Jesus. He replied, "Let it be so now, for thus it is fitting for us to fulfill all righteousness." I immersed Jesus into the water and when He resurfaced the clouds rolled away and the heavens above opened up and the spirit of God descended like a dove, resting upon Him. A loud and commanding voice from above declared, "This is my beloved Son with whom I am well pleased."

He is finally here. Months and years of proclaiming the coming Messiah and now it has come true. This all took place during the 15th year of the reign of Tiberius Caesar; the governor of Judea, a ruthless man who went by the name of Pontius Pilate. Herod was the Jewish tetrarch of Galilee and Annias and Caiaphas were the high priests. It was kind of a political mess, so to speak, but I usually didn't bother with that, except the time I told Herod that it was unlawful for him to have Herodias, his brother's wife. He didn't take kindly to it. However, my mission wasn't to get wrapped up in the political scene but rather to keep spreading the word of the coming King. I'm sure that didn't sit well with the political elites.

Jesus was becoming pretty popular, and His fame was far-reaching. It was exciting to see the works of Jesus and the fruits of my calling being born out right in front of me. Deep down, I always knew that my message and ministry would one day be the death of me, still I wasn't ready when the guards showed up on Herod's birthday.

Day's before Herod's elite guards had seized me with brutal force, spitting on me, pulling my beard and peppering my kidneys with punch after punch. I resisted. It wasn't in my nature not to put up a struggle, but ultimately I was overpowered and bound with rope pulled so tightly around my wrists and ankles that blood trickled down my arms and legs. The ride to my holding cell was uncomfortable to say the least, and then to say that I was thrown into prison would be an understatement.

My mission, which was to proclaim Christ, was clear, but it wasn't easy. While a great party was going on in the royal courtyard in honor of Herod's birthday, I made some small talk and then continued with my mission, conversing with a young guard. I think I was making progress in helping him to see the Light when an older centurion stepped in, interrupted our conversation and told me that my time had come to an end. I wrote in my journal one last time, which, remarkably, they had let me keep. I wrote on the last page:

> Beheading?
> Crucifixion?
> I must decrease, so that Christ may increase!

I AM LIKE JOHN THE BAPTIST

I am like John the Baptist, sometimes. I am a man who knows his ultimate mission and who is willing to go all out for it, but also I am a man who doubts my calling and so often is looking for a new calling. I confuse myself with my own thoughts as I try to understand my path and how best to fulfill my mission. I am a man who needs to learn to decrease so that Jesus Christ may increase. John understood this all too well.

One Sunday, my former pastor encouraged the congregation to come up with a one-sentence mission statement that best described what they felt God was calling them to do. For example, John the Baptist's motto would've been, "I am less—Christ is more" because John knew his earthly calling was to let people know that Christ was the Messiah. After much prayer and thought, my personal mission statement became: "To motivate, encourage, and strengthen others to live for Jesus Christ." This sentence gives my ministry calling more focus and clarity and allows me to better stay on track as to what God has called me to do for His kingdom.

Before I understood my mission statement, I was all over the board with ministry. I was easily distracted and pulled in many directions, which had an impact on the effectiveness of my ministry. Now my mission is much clearer, allowing me to stay focused on what God has called me to do. God has refined my thoughts, changed my direction, provided peace and helped me to understand how I can effectively use my gifts in combination with my mission. It all started with prayer, self-examination, and the help of a pastor who placed the thought in my head.

For men willing to do this, a next step would be to go to family and friends and ask them to put in writing a list of their strengths and weaknesses, citing both positive and negative character traits. Or, you could send out a survey and receive anonymous responses from your friends and family members with their honest replies. It may not always be fun to hear some of the things that they say about you, but ultimately it will help you better understand who you are. Your friends may tell you that you are a strong encourager but are weak in mercy, or your family may tell you that you are not a great administrator but that you connect well with people. Whatever they say will reveal a lot about you, and that will help you develop a strategy for ministry that fits with who you are.

Understand that over time our strengths and weaknesses can change as we mature and improve in a particular area. Or we may choose to neglect them. Remember to saturate this process and all its steps in prayer so that God can use these people and tools to help form and shape us.

Other methods to help identify our traits might be to talk with a pastor, meet with an elder, take a spiritual-gift test or attend a class on understanding spiritual gifts. Each of us must find what works best for us and then dig deeper. There is no set formula for how we come to grips with how God has designed us and what He wants from us. Each man's mission won't be exactly like mine or anyone else's. Embrace the fact that God made each one of us to be unique, different from everyone else.

FEAR IS A DISTRACTION

Fear is a great paralyzer. When we allow our trepidations to limit us, our gifts are going to be rendered less useful unless we can learn to overcome those fears. Anxiety! Apprehension! Dread! Trepidation! All are synonyms for the word "fear." The Encarta English Dictionary states that fear "is an unpleasant feeling of anxiety or apprehension caused by the presence or anticipation of danger. Or it can be an idea, thought or other entity that causes feelings of fear."

Going on mission for God means that we will have opposition. One of our enemy's greatest weapons is fear. When I allow unpleasant feelings, insecure thoughts, and other outside sources of fear to creep into my heart, then the enemy has already won that battle. I can't allow fear to discourage or distract me from the mission God has called me to. In battle, a soldier is always moving forward. Occasionally he may have to hunker down and brace for the barrage of an enemy's attacks, but he never wants to lose ground. We are to stand firm and strong.

The antonym for fear is assurance. In our Christian walk, it means that God has given us numerous promises that everything will work out. God's assurance should give us the confidence we need to be free from uncertainty and fear.

> *And we know that for those who love God all things work together for good, for those who are called according to his purpose* (Romans 8:28).

Fear is not from God. He has given us a spirit of power, love, and self-control. He has also sent us a helper, the Holy Spirit, to guide, direct, convict, and to bring us comfort in times of need. God wants us to prosper and to be bold, confident, and fully trusting that He is genuinely on our side. We need to stop letting fear rule our lives when God is, without a doubt, on our side and wants only what is best for us.

> *But, as it is written, "What no eye has seen, nor ear heard, nor the heart of man imagined, what God has prepared for those who love him" (1 Corinthians 2:9).*

The evil one wants to keep us from fulfilling God's plan for our lives. He wants to steal our identity, trash our reputation and to render us useless. There are many ways in which the evil one can negatively influence us, but in terms of our calling he is going to focus on making us feel unqualified. He is a liar! We are absolutely qualified because God chose us, and nothing can take that away. Not even the evil one's lies, our own insecurities, nor the acceptance of others can disqualify us from doing God's will for our lives. Fear can be crippling and it also can be destructive if we allow it the freedom to roll around in our hearts and minds.

Over the years I've learned that my calling has nothing to do with pleasing man or even coming to fully understand that calling, but successfully completing my mission has everything to do with pleasing God and serving Him. I may not be the most qualified person, at least in my own eyes, but I am qualified because God says so and He is the ultimate authority. He will not ask me to do anything that He Himself is not willing to equip me to do.

Whether someone is a weak man or a reluctant misfit, God

loves that man and has a plan for that life. We follow Him and commit with passion to the adventure God has called us to take. We are called to surrender our fears, our gifts, and our lives to Him. I can guarantee that whatever God chooses for a man to do, God will be there with him every step of the way.

When I was in eighth grade I was often included in the crazy adventures of my brother and his gang of high school buddies. The youth group was led by a young man in his twenties who liked to play as much as we did. He was the only reason all of our parents let us hang out with him; he was mature and responsible, or so they thought.

My first concept of being on mission was introduced to me in the form of Army Ranger School, but not the one you are thinking. The boys in the youth group set up a Ranger battalion and would dress in army gear. They would go out into the woods on make-believe patrol missions, battles, or games of capture the flag. It was highly classified and only on a need-to-know basis. I was invited along on a few occasions as a Jr. Ranger and, if I handled myself well there was room to advance into becoming a Sr. Ranger. I put in my time, showed myself well in make-believe battle, and I came out as the only middle school student to achieve Sr. Ranger status. I even have a certificate that proves it. The reason for my advancement was that I was poly-missionic; basically, I went on enough adventures to earn my promotion.

As I entered high school, these Sr. Rangers grew out of the make-believe war because a new sport called paintball was emerging, and this group was destined to be a part of it. Our make-believe adventures grew into a more realistic endeavor, one that would leave many of us with welts and bloody lips because we never thought of wearing facemasks. We got lucky when we used BB guns in battle, and we figured paint was much softer, or so we thought, until a purple ball of paint came flying at us at three hundred feet per second.

After many wars in the local woods, it was time to take our low-level standard gear and our backwoods skill to the next level, and we signed up for a regional tournament that was being held in the sticks of Ohio. About a dozen of us from Michigan jumped in cars and took off, excited about cleaning up the competition. After all, this was promoted as a stock competition, so no constant air, large-capacity loaders, etc. were allowed. Our standard pistols that held about ten rounds and one small CO_2 canister would serve us well.

It came time for the tournament, and when we arrived we were notified that the rules had been changed and that this tournament would now allow constant-air, big hoppers that held hundreds of rounds of ammo. We could also purchase from them any other extra gear that we would like to have. We would be going up against teams like the Bushmasters and other similarly cool military-team names. Oh, and there was also a team everyone hated whose members dressed and played like Nazis. It was at this point that my mission, which was to come down and have fun, needed to quickly change since we were going to be out-armed. Sure enough, during the first game our entire team was obliterated in about ten minutes as all of us were shot while reloading after firing off approximately ten rounds. Needless to say, our standings in the tournament were not going to go well that day.

After the first game, we emptied our wallets and paid the additional expense to get some accessories for our guns in hopes that would give us a chance at success. We lost our next game and were officially out of the tournament. But with a renewed sense of mission and what it took to win, we cleaned up in the consolation games.

I went into my paintball mission without any real understanding of what it took to become victorious. As a team we were unprepared.

But John the Baptist always knew his mission from the very beginning and he was completely sold out on fulfilling it, even if it meant living a life that was different from everyone else's. John said, "I am not the Christ, but I have been sent before Him." John's mission was always to prepare the way for Jesus and he never allowed himself to get caught up in the success of his ministry and the followers that he was gaining; he was spreading the coming Good News.

What does God expect of us? Well, in any mission it is important to know what it is we are trying to accomplish. What is the end goal? The mission may have multiple objectives, but they all work together to accomplish a specific goal. For example: God asks a few things from us while we are here on this earth, but all that He asks leads us back to Him.

First, we are to love God with all of our heart, mind, and strength. Second, we are to love others, putting their needs before our own needs. Third, He wants us to care for the poor, orphaned, and widowed. Fourth, God wants us to reach the lost for Him and spread the message of Jesus around the world. Fifth, He wants us to build each other up so that we can be spiritually strong and handle the battle we find ourselves in, hence one of the purposes of attending a church.

These are all objectives within the mission for our lives which are all designed to bring us to our ultimate goal and that is to bring honor and glory to God in all that we do. Along the way He may give us some other task that only we can do but that may not necessarily fit into one of these major categories; if it is from God, then we just go with it and see His sovereignty at work.

Remember that all missions require some readiness and preparation before engaging in them. If this doesn't happen then the likelihood of success is minimal. If you are a pastor, you must work at preaching, continuing to improve and reading books to learn how to communicate better, or by watching other speakers and taking note of pacing, eye contact, and other communication techniques in order to improve.

If you are a worship leader you probably are listening to popular musical groups for quality songs and meaningful lyrics, or searching the hymnals for a sacred gem. You are watching other bands to see what works and what doesn't and making sure you balance your Sunday praise and worship to be honoring to God and not just a show.

If God has called you to be a light within your workplace, then you have an obligation to be ready and prepared. You should be reading your Bible daily or weekly. You should be in constant prayer, memorizing some verses and engaged in some form of devotions or research of topics that may come up in conversation.

How will you succeed in communicating the truth of Christ if you don't even know what the Bible says? How will you defend the faith? Do you understand Christian apologetics? If not, be prepared. It's amazing how God will use what we learn from our daily/weekly studies at just the right time. If you want to be on-mission for God, that means you must be prepared.

Finally, to be on-mission requires the courage to engage your heart and step into action to fulfill God's purposes. Being just a hearer of the Word of God is not good enough without also doing what the Word says. Christ's church, not by design, has become a group of misfits who seem reluctant to answer God's call into ministry, or in serving others.

We've become reluctant to use our spiritual gifts, reluctant to love others, to forgive others, to give of our time, and we are reluctant to give of our first fruits (our money). Some in the church have become reluctant in willingness to move, if necessary, especially forward. But, most importantly, many in the church are reluctant to trust God with their whole heart and to share the message of Jesus.

To be on-mission means we have to have the courage to engage our hearts and to believe in the mission we've been called to.

God chooses weak men to fulfill His plans. King David was a shepherd, an adulterer, a liar and a murderer — yet God chose him because he was a man after God's own heart. Moses was a murderer, a fugitive, and a shepherd. Saul misused his education, his status, his Jewish lineage, his biblical teachings, and his misguided zeal to be a persecutor of Christians. Esther was an orphan used by God to save the Jews from total destruction. Rahab was a prostitute used to rescue and save the spies at Jericho. Jeremiah was a youth when God called him to be a prophet. Samson was a ladies' man, yet God used him as one of the judges to punish the Philistines. Jacob was a manipulator, but was used immensely in shaping the future of Israel. And Peter was a fisherman with an innate ability to mess things up even though he was trying to do the right thing.

John the Baptist would've made a great character on the popular television show *Duck Dynasty.* John's mission was to decrease so that Christ could increase. My mission is to motivate, encourage, and strengthen others to live for Christ through written and verbal communication.

What's your mission?

> *The voice of one crying in the wilderness: Prepare the way of the Lord; make his paths straight (Isaiah 40:3).*

> *Go therefore and make disciples of all nations, baptizing them in the name of the Father and of the Son and of the Holy Spirit, teaching them to observe all that I have commanded you. And behold, I am with you always, to the end of the age (Matthew 28:19–20).*

John the Baptist—Areas of weakness	How God used John the Baptist
· He was a wilderness man	· As a messenger
· He had little to his name	· To prepare the coming of Christ
· He had no position or title	· As an evangelist
	· To baptize Jesus
	· To baptize others and to help lead them to repentance
	· As a martyr

LIFE APPLICATION QUESTIONS:

(Read Matthew 3, 11, 14 and John 3 to learn more about the life and ministry of John the Baptist.)

1. What set John the Baptist apart from others?
2. Was the mission of John the Baptist a part-time endeavor for him?
3. In what ways did John the Baptist fulfill his ministry calling?

> *Being on-mission for God doesn't mean you have to grow a beard, but it does mean that your life and focus on yourself will need to decrease while your faith must increase.*

4. What did John the Baptist do to deserve imprisonment and beheading?
5. Has God called you to do something for Him? If so, how do you think others will treat you as you attempt to fulfill your calling?
6. If God hasn't called you to do anything yet, then what do you think you need to do to be ready to be on-mission for God?

LIFE HAS SO MUCH MORE PURPOSE WHEN WE ARE ON-MISSION FOR GOD.

Chapter Fourteen

ETERNITY

Was I dreaming? Is this real? Am I projecting?

The menacing vale stood before me; I felt covered in a shadow of death. There was no turning back, so I stood to face the valley below with much trepidation. My mind was cloudy as to the circumstances that brought me there, but deep down in my soul I knew I must travel this route.

The narrow path wound its way down the mountainside. It was rocky and difficult to navigate. My badly-dented armor was barely hanging on and I'm not sure it would even protect me in case of another attack. I had fought in too many battles and my armor had always protected me; my sword was still as sharp as ever. But what I was about to face didn't compare to the other skirmishes I had encountered. I was now in the valley of death; only one thing could save me from the peril that I was about to face.

The deeper I descended into this vale the darker and more ominous the air around me became. I reached the bottom and looked at the narrow path that split the dark timber awaiting my arrival. I cautiously stepped into the silent forest, the only sound coming from my own steps. The trees were like giants, scorched black, not from fire but from something else. I couldn't detect any critters but there was movement in the shadows.

I looked back toward the mountain and could see the snow resting peacefully on its peak. The dark timber was closing in around me and the light from where I had come was slowly diminishing. It wouldn't be long before the light from the entrance had been extinguished. The path continued to weave its way through the dark forest leading me on a journey that I must take alone.

A loud blood-curdling shriek pierced the air and something zoomed over my head, just missing me and causing me to fall to the ground. More screeches began to fill the woods. Some were close, others far away. They were quickly multiplying. I drew my sword.

Suddenly, the screaming stopped and the shadowy figures retreated a short distance away. Pairs of glowing red eyes seemed to be perched in the trees staring down at me. They looked at me, then farther up the trail and then back at me. Something had caused them to retreat, but what? I could see off in the distance a small purple light; it was coming my way. The closer it came, the brighter the light grew, with white on the inside and an iridescent purple haze on the outer edges. The shrieks came again as the shadowy figures took flight. The approaching glow revealed the silhouettes of large-winged creatures fleeing deeper into the dark timber.

I stood my ground, remarkably unafraid. As the light drew closer, its radiance caused me to squint. When my eyes adjusted to the brightness, I could see the figure of a man. Yet I knew I was in the presence of something greater. The man's appearance was that of a simple shepherd, but kingly in nature, and he carried a stick. His voice was soft and gentle, but boomed a majestic quality I had not heard before. He said, "Fear no evil and do not be afraid though you walk through the valley of the shadow of death. for my rod and my staff will comfort you."

"Jesus?"

"Yes, son" he said as he approached and gave me a hug.

"Put your sword back in your sheath. You won't need that where you're going." Jesus walked with me the rest of the way through the vale of death as a father would walk with his young son.

We left the woods, and standing before me was heaven, a glorious place too beautiful to describe. We climbed the steps to the grand balcony of a majestic mansion. People filled the area, mingling and talking and seemingly waiting in line. Jesus told me to wait until my name was called and then disappeared.

Those around me wore shiny new armor with helmets, swords, and breastplates that looked like they were brand new. My armor was dirty, dented, broken, and barely held together. My body was beaten and battered from all the battles I had encountered. What place do I have among these soldiers?

The grand balcony was buzzing with anticipation and filled with warm greetings and voices welcoming each other to heaven. A voice like the sound of thunder bellowed. Everyone was instantly silent. A hushed reverence was on display and the people respected the moment. The angelic but powerful voice called out my name and instructed me to come to the front of the line at the opposite end of the balcony.

I walked with a limp and was slightly hunched over from all the warfare I had experienced in my day. I slowly moved in the direction of the voice and noticed everyone looking at me. I was slightly embarrassed because I looked like such a mess. The voice boomed again, "Make way for the great warrior!" As I approached the front, the crowd separated and made a path leading up to two large pearly gates. Standing in front of them was a muscular angelic greeter towering above even the tallest of men on earth. He stood next to a giant shimmering gold and granite stand. On top of the stand lay a giant, ancient-looking book about three feet wide by three feet high.

I stopped about ten feet in front of him just so I wouldn't have to look straight up to meet his gaze. The bands strapping the shield to my left arm snapped and the shield clanged noisily on the ground as it bounced at my feet. The room was silent, but the angel just smiled at me, winked and chuckled. "What's your name soldier?" he asked. I told him, and then he opened the book to see if it was listed. He found it and read it out loud.

The giant pearly gates behind him began to open and I was instructed to go on through. I said, "What about the others?" He replied, "The first shall be last and the last shall be first!" As I walked beyond the gates they began to shut behind me and then I heard that familiar voice again, "Well done, my good and faithful servant!"

I WANT TO BE A GOOD AND FAITHFUL SERVANT

I want to be the man who gets back up every time he is knocked down. I want to be the person who puts it all on the line for Christ. I desire to finish strong and be welcomed with those glorious words from Jesus, "Well done! My good and faithful servant."

A man's time living on the earth is very short; time continues moving forward. Our significance in this world is equivalent to being a single droplet of rain in a tropical thunderstorm, a grain of sand lying at the bottom of the Grand Canyon, a piece of seaweed floating in the Pacific Ocean. Yet, we have importance.

There are no guarantees in life; death is not prejudiced and my status in life has no bearing on the day I revert back to dust. Would the earth stop spinning if I were not on it? James 4:14 reminds us, "Yet you do not know what tomorrow will bring. What is your life? For you are a mist that appears for a little time and then vanishes."

My mother was approximately fifty-four years of age when she was diagnosed with breast cancer; she was buried just before her sixty-fourth birthday. She fought hard and as a result she was able to see and experience the births and the young lives of all of her thirteen grandchildren, seven of whom she would never have known if not for God's graciousness in giving her those ten extra years.

My mother was a person who acknowledged the existence of God but never turned her heart over to the Lord until, as a young married woman, she came to know Jesus Christ as her personal Lord and Savior. If she were here today, she would tell you about her sometimes rebellious attitude toward God. She didn't like it when someone told her what to do, and often that meant even God. She would struggle. She would resist, but she always went to God in prayer and, in reading her Bible, always ended up submitting and letting God have His way in her life.

She liked to have fun, but we often joked with her about her need to relax. We had many other family jokes at her expense. She was competitive when it came to games and wasn't against changing the rules at the last minute if it suited her. But, most importantly, she was a great mom. She made a big impact on many people's lives and is a huge inspiration to me when the going gets tough.

To this day I still remember sitting in the hospital room with my brother and seeing her sit up in bed, look us in the eyes and tell us she was done fighting. In unison, we both said that it was okay. She had fought so valiantly. Others probably would have given up well before Marianne Tison did with the kind of road blocks she constantly faced. She was a strong Dutch woman, filled with a stubbornness that would serve her well while sick, but even she knew when her time had come to an end.To my friends I say, your time is right now. Don't waste it.

Each of us is a gift to this world, just like the lone snowflake that is needed to transform a dull brown place into a winter wonderland. I know that I am created with specific dimensions, special characteristics, and precise attributes, all given for the purpose of completing the Artist's masterpiece. Individual elements placed perfectly and used properly help me to become a part of something bigger than myself.

Preoccupation with the things of this earth can keep me from fulfilling the plans God has for me. I often get sidetracked and lose my way. I feel that God's commandments, rules, statutes, and testimonies can be easily forgotten. The instructions Jesus gave about loving God and my neighbors get replaced with loving myself. My time and money are spent on my own interests rather than on feeding the poor, supporting missions, or serving God's church.

God calls us men to love our families, yet we can spend great amounts of time in the woods hunting or attending sporting events, all the while neglecting the needs of our spouse and children. Climbing the corporate ladder or binge entertainment can become a man's focus. Too easily men like me are distracted by the material things of our culture. We become hoarders and time wasters at the expense of the basic tenets of our faith and of our family. I'm discovering that enjoying life requires balance and good stewardship of my time and resources.

When I focus on the things of God, even under imperfect conditions, I find that my life is fulfilling and rewarding. Concentrating on the spiritual objectives of God may not provide an easier life, but it is a happier life filled with hope, peace, kindness, joy, and much-needed strength during times of difficulty. Without God my life would be a constant struggle, a never-ending fight to find peace.

I am often like the man who goes to the Grand Canyon to hike but is always looking at his feet as he walks; he misses out on the gorgeous scenery. I want to stop looking at my feet and look to heaven. That is where the real beauty of living on this earth lies.

Most people are living for today with barely a thought of eternity —Billy Graham.

Set your minds on things that are above, not on things that are on earth (*Colossians* 3:2).

Areas of weakness	What I should do
· Focusing on earthly things	· Focus on heavenly things

LIFE APPLICATION QUESTIONS:

(Read Colossians 3 for more on this topic.)

1. List in order of priority the top five things that are important to you on earth.

2. List in order of priority the top five spiritual things that are important to you here on earth.

3. Look through both lists and place them in order of importance to you. Be honest in your placement, one being the ultimate priority and ten being the least.

> *God wants to bless us and to provide for us, but He doesn't call us to a life of luxury; He calls us to a ministry of love, service, and sacrifice.*

4. Based on your top ten list, if God were to look at your list would you be embarrassed for Him to read it?

5. Is your time here on earth best represented by thinking about heavenly things or earthly things?

6. If your honest answer was earthly things, then what changes do you need to make to help you develop more of an eternal perspective?

OUR TIME HERE ON EARTH IS SHORT.

EPILOGUE

When I was reading through the Bible to find great stories that would complement the theme of this book, I came across the story of Esther. I was greatly intrigued by her story. In the end I couldn't apply the story directly to these chapters but I want to leave readers with a final thought from Esther's story. Reading the whole story in the book of Esther in the Old Testament will be an enriching experience.

King Ahasuerus, who reigned over 127 provinces from India to Ethiopia, threw a party to show off his greatness. His queen, Vashti, was beautiful and the king wanted to present her to the people and to the princes who had gathered for the celebrations. He wanted to brag and show off her beauty. She refused to come out and the king was enraged. His anger burned so much that he decided to replace her with a new queen.

Enter Esther, a Jew, who was ravishing to look at. Ultimately, she was selected to become the new queen. God positioned her into a kingdom of political turmoil. The king's minions were busy at work plotting the destruction of the Jews. Queen Esther's heritage remained a secret; however, the plot against her people was being put into motion.

Queen Esther was now confronted with a difficult decision. She could go to the king to tell him of this plot and hope to save her people, but if she went to him uninvited she could be put to death. She needed to find favor with him. It had been thirty days since the king had last called her, so she was reluctant to approach him. After all, who was she? She was just an orphan girl, a pretty Jew, without many gifts or talents. How could she make a difference?

I love her Uncle Mordecai's response to her when he said, "For if you keep silent at this time, relief and deliverance will rise for the Jews from another place, but you and your father's house will perish. And who knows whether you have not come to the kingdom for such a time as this?"

That thought penetrated Esther's heart, and her response was to risk her life in order to save her people. She visited the king and she found favor with him. Her life was spared and she was presented the opportunity to expose the plot of the man who wanted to destroy the Jews. The story ends well for all—except for the man behind the plot who doesn't deserve to be mentioned.

Know that God is working in your life. He is shaping you to become the person that you are destined to be. Your past is shaping your future. Even youthful inexperience is not an excuse. The fact you may not be an eloquent speaker is not even a consideration. God knows your faults, your weaknesses, and your sins. Yet He chooses you. Who knows; maybe God has called you for such a time as this?

ACKNOWLEDGMENTS

I want to thank the following people for supporting this writing project. Without their prayers, encouragement, and contributions this book wouldn't have happened. I know that most, if not all of these people, do not want to be recognized for their support, but I would like to follow the example and words of the apostle Paul when he wrote in 1 Corinthians 16:17, "I rejoice at the coming of Stephanas and Fortunatus and Achaicus, because they have made up for your absence, for they refreshed my spirit as well as yours. Give recognition to such men."

Each of you in one way or another has refreshed my spirit and has always supported my ministries. Thank you very much!

Sarah Tison—a precious gift from God.

Larry Tison—for giving me a life filled with love and so many great memories.

Charles and Winifred Kemler—my biggest supporters and the best in-laws ever.

Ken Tison—for being an awesome brother, mentor, and giving me the idea for the story of chapter 14—Eternity.

Roger Palms—for all of your hard work in fine-tuning and bringing out the best in my writing.

Carrie Thompson—for all of the time you spent managing this project and putting it all together.

Andy Scheer—for reviewing my first manuscript and for coming up with the tag-line: Hope for the Men God Chooses.

Jerry B. Jenkins—for your commitment in developing new authors.

Tom Craig and Faithconnector—for your support of my ministries by providing me with great websites.

And a special thank you to all of the other people who helped make this book a possibility:

Dan and Debbie Willson
Mickey and Lisa Weston
Jeff and Jenny Mclanson
Dennis Weinand
Dana and Donelle Tison
Scott and Theresa Bills
Robert Saunders
William and Tracy Gottschalk
Joe Broussard
Trevor Ruble
Dallas Jenkins
Ed and Esther Roden
Mark McElrath
Jon and Mimi Shackelford
Jerry Hammarlund
H.L. Hussman
Kevin and Sheila Shorkey
Wally and Carolyn Parshall
Jimmy Carter (No, not that one)
Bill Bronkema
Ken "The Kenadian" Harris
Luke Cyrus—check out his music

To learn more about Mike Tison's speaking ministry

and his other books please visit:

MissionAmped.com